PRAISE FOR
Dress Codes for Small Towns

"Courtney Stevens bats for the fences from the first page, capturing the complicated love of family, the simple love of home, the sustaining love of friendship, the quiet, steady love that comes from faith, the messy love that blooms between two people, and the most difficult love of all: the ability to know and love yourself for who you are. I dare you not to love this book."
—Stephanie Appell, manager of books for young readers, Parnassus Books

"No one writes family and heart and the South like Courtney Stevens. *Dress Codes for Small Towns* is a poetic love letter to the complexities of teenage identity and the frustrations of growing up in a place where everything fits in a box—except you. This book cannot be contained."
—David Arnold, author of *Kids of Appetite*

"Courtney Stevens carries us into the best kind of mess: deep friendships, small-town southern gossip, unexpected garage art, and unfolding romantic identity. When I finished *Dress Codes for Small Towns*, you could hear my smile squeak from way across the room."
—Jaye Robin Brown, author of *Georgia Peaches and Other Forbidden Fruit*

"Courtney Stevens delivers a cherished gift for our middle grade and high school readers. The gift of friendship. The gift of safe places. The gift of love. And, most important, the gift of acceptance."
—Julie R. Stokes, literacy coordinator, Dalton Middle School, Dalton, Georgia

"With *Dress Codes for Small Towns*, Courtney Stevens firmly reasserts herself as a master storyteller of young adult fiction, crafting stories bursting with humor, heart, and the deepest sort of empathy."
—Jeff Zentner, William C. Morris Award winner for *The Serpent King*

Dress Codes for Small Towns

Courtney Stevens

HARPER TEEN
An Imprint of HarperCollinsPublishers

HarperTeen is an imprint of HarperCollins Publishers.

Dress Codes for Small Towns
Copyright © 2017 by Courtney Stevens

Library of Congress Control Number: 2016949991
ISBN 978-0-06-239851-2

Typography by Torborg Davern
This book is set in 12-point Dante

17 18 19 20 21   PC/LSCH   10 9 8 7 6 5 4 3 2 1
❖
First Edition

For CJ, PKs, and Tomboys
1 Samuel 18:1

THE SHORT PART
before
PART ONE

That's the way things come clear. All of a sudden.
And then you realize how obvious they've been all along.
—MADELEINE L'ENGLE, *The Arm of the Starfish*

Three-hundred-year-old oaks were good for two things: hiding from playground fights and kingdom-watching. Billie McCaffrey climbed skyward and settled into a sprawling fork to observe her classmates. Over by the four square concrete slab, Janie Lee Miller sat cross-legged with her nose in a library copy of *A Wrinkle in Time*. Across the field, Woods Carrington was campaigning for a kickball game. Just below, two third-grade boys, Mash and Fifty, fought over a fourth-grade girl in blue bows and light-pink sunglasses. Other boys swung from the monkey bars while a herd of girls huddled, giggling and happy, around the adults. Their teacher, the center of the girls' commotion, was dressed in a plain denim jumper and wore a bouquet of smiles. She produced from an ugly black handbag her newly awarded Corn Dolly. "Ooooh," said the little girls. "Ahhhh," said other teachers, who asked if they could hold the doll. They treated that decorated corn husk like Billie's daddy treated a Bible.

Billie oooohed and ahhhhed like everyone else, her voice barely above a whisper. No one even glanced up.

Before the end of that school year, Billie had learned from her daddy that if she wanted friends, she couldn't stay in tree forks. So she stopped climbing up, up and away, and befriended every boy in her grade by either brute force or voodoo charm. Woods, Billie's new best friend, claimed it was her kickball skills. By God, that girl could kick a ball farther into Mr. Vilmer's cornfield than anyone in the class. Even the most competitive boys loved her for it. The girls were a different story. They didn't quite know what to do with her. And Billie didn't know what to do with them.

Late summer brought water-gun fights, fishing at the quarry, and biking to and from the dam to skip rocks along the mirrored surface of Kentucky Lake. All this good fortune sparked a happy question from Woods.

"Hey, B, will you come to mine and Janie Lee's wedding tomorrow?"

Billie chomped on an apple they'd smuggled from Tawny Jacobs's orchard. Juice ringed her lips. "Do I have to wear a dress?"

"Nah," Woods said. "You're my best man."

After passing the last bite to Woods and wiping her mouth with her shirtsleeve, she considered his request. Seemed fair. Seemed important. "Sounds good to me," she said, even though it sounded worse than awful.

"Promise?" He looked concerned that she might go back to her tree-climbing, avoiding-everyone ways.

"Promise."

She made the mistake of spit shaking. That night she asked her dad, "Will I go to hell if I break a promise?" He'd assured her that hell did not work that way. But she didn't know which way hell worked yet, so she tore up all the notes she'd written asking Woods not to marry Janie Lee.

The next day, Woods Carrington stood behind one of those sprawling playground oaks and wed Janie Lee Miller with a grape Ring Pop and a peck on the lips.

Billie wore her cleanest jeans and stood by Woods's side.

She looked up to her old perch and thought this friend thing was very hard.

PART ONE

HEXAGONS ARE TRIANGLES

First say to yourself what you would be;
and then do what you have to do.

—EPICTETUS

1

I'm waffling on my tombstone inscription today. *Elizabeth McCaffrey, born 1999—d. ? R.I.P.: She found trouble.* Or. *Elizabeth McCaffrey, born 1999—d. ? IN LOVING MEMORY: Trouble found her.*

"This is a bad idea," Janie Lee tells me. Which is her way of saying we're going to get caught.

"We will *not* be contained by a grubby youth room and pointless rules," I reply.

Janie Lee peers down the hallway. There's no sign of my dad, but her expression indicates she's voting for retreat. The dingy carpet beneath her feet is patterned with repeating arrows that all point the way back to our assigned sleeping room.

I tickle-poke her in the ribs. She giggles and leans into the tickle instead of away. "I'll protect you," I tell her.

That's enough prompting for her to skitter down the hall with me—two handsome thieves on a wayward mission.

We stand in front of a door labeled *Youth Suite 201.* It's 3:12 a.m. Janie Lee is wearing a sweet pink sweatshirt, flannel pants, and UGGs, which always make me ugh. I am wearing a camo T-shirt, jeans I stole from Mash last weekend, and combat boots that I found at a local army surplus. Clothes I can sleep in. And, well, clothes I can live in.

Elizabeth McCaffrey, born 1999—d. ? IN LOVING MEMORY: She died in her boots.

I perform the prearranged triple knock.

Davey props open the door, and behind him the rest of our boys offer various greetings. He's the newest of the gang and we're all still learning him. There's an awkward pause while we work out whether we're supposed to fist-bump or shoulder-punch or hug. I up-nod, and that seems to be acceptable enough for him to duplicate.

I turn my attention to the rest of the room. I've just noticed that Einstein the Whiteboard is leaning against the mini-fridge when something hits me. It's Woods, tackling me to the decades-old carpet.

"Hello to you, too," I say from beneath him.

He licks my face like a Saint Bernard and then pretends to do an elaborate wrestling move that I don't evade. (Even though I could.) Without warning, a two-person dog pile becomes a six-person dog pile. Davey hesitates, then lands near the top. He must be learning us a little. Boys really are such affectionate assholes. I am crushed at the bottom and Janie Lee is half-balanced on top of Davey's back.

"Love sandwich," she mouths at me.

It is. It's not. It's more. Labeling and limiting something as big as us feels somewhat impossible, but usually we call ourselves the Hexagon. On the account that sixsome sounds kinky and stupid.

"Up! We're crushing Billie," Woods says, because he's always directing traffic.

Fifty farts in Davey's face in a momentous fashion, and just like that, the jokes begin and the dog pile ends, boys sprawling onto the two couches as if it never happened. I digest the scene as I slouch against the door. Boys. My boys. I've been collecting them like baseball cards since third grade.

Woods. He's not pretty, but he's stark and golden and green like a cornfield under noon sunlight. Tennis shoes; low-cut, grass-stained socks; ropey calf muscles; blond leg hair; khaki shorts; aqua polo; and an unmatching St. Louis Cardinals hat tamping down floofy blondish-brown curls: he is these things. He is so much more. I know exactly what he'll look like in thirty years when he's sitting on our porch drinking peppermint tea.

Davey, elfin and punkish in smeared eyeliner, sits next to his cousin Mash, who looks nothing much like him. Fifty always appears a bit smarmy, and tonight is no exception. His dark hair is oily and he hasn't shaved in a week. Janie Lee sits slightly apart, cross-legged and petite in a papasan chair. She takes up about as much room as a ghost. Then me. Knees up. Chin up. Happy. Taking their mischief like the gift that it is.

Some lock-ins are for staying up all night and playing shit-tastic games. This one is for parental convenience. The youth group is cleaning up Vilmer's Barn tomorrow—early prep for the upcoming Harvest Festival—and Dad didn't want to run a shuttle at six a.m. Tyson Vilmer, barn owner, patriarch of Otters Holt, grandfather of Mash and Davey, will be there waiting with his enormous smile and incredible enthusiasm. Despite the fact that we were supposed to be in separate rooms and asleep by two a.m., I am pretty damn excited to help. Two a.m. bedtime was wishful thinking on my father's part. We are not true hellcats, but the Hexagon is particularly bad at *supposed to* when we're all under one roof.

The other four can't decide who will open the meeting: Woods or me.

I copy Dad's southern drawl and say, "Let's start with glads, sads, and sorries and then say a prayer." They all laugh, except for Davey, who hasn't been to enough Wednesday night Bible studies to get the joke. I gesture to the writing on Einstein the Whiteboard. "Dudes and Dudette, I predict this lock-in ends poorly."

Woods will hear nothing of my prophecy. Einstein is among Woods's favorite things on the planet—a medium-sized board that technically belongs to the youth group but practically belongs to him. Woods developed leadership skills in utero, and he thinks in dry-erase bullet points. Currently, Einstein says: THINGS TO DO WITH A CHURCH MICROWAVE. Five bullets follow, and most of them look like a one-way trip to a stark-raving Brother Scott McCaffrey, my father.

In the bottom corner, someone has drawn a sketch of a Corn Dolly being lifted on high by a stick figure. They've labeled the stick figure *Billie McCaffrey*, which makes me label them all idiots. The joke is so old it has wrinkles.

A Corn Dolly is only a corn husk that has been folded and tucked and tied into the shape of a doll. In the town of Otters Holt, the mayor handpicks this husk on the morning of the Harvest Festival, which is an annual event the town treats like Christmas-meets-the-Resurrection. The dolly is then assembled and bestowed during the middle of the Sadie Hawkins dance to the most deserving woman of the year.

Hence, the joke.

"Ha. Ha. Ha," I say, slow clapping.

Woods is positive THINGS TO DO WITH A CHURCH MICROWAVE is suitable 3:15 a.m. material. "You say ends badly. I say ends brilliantly," he says.

Fifty has an opinion on the matter. "The only thing far-fetched is Billie actually winning a Corn Dolly." He laughs at himself. Too hard. We are often forced to forgive this failing since his facial hair allows him a fake ID, which allows us the beer that comes along with that privilege.

I'm eye-rolling. "You asshole." Just because it's true doesn't mean he needs to say it.

Fifty stands up as if to challenge me while Janie Lee buries her face in the nearest pillow and reminds us that teenagers don't, won't ever win the Corn Dolly—Gloria Nix, twenty-three, was the youngest.

I wave Fifty forward with both hands, ready to wrestle him down.

"Back to Einstein," Woods announces before Fifty and I go for a real row. This may have happened a time or two in the past.

"Back to Einstein," everyone, including Fifty, choruses. The merriment rises to previous levels.

"This microwave thing." I point to the first bullet point: *Cook Pineapple Bob.* "I do like it."

Woods is beaming proudly. "He's had a good life."

I agree. Pineapple Bob is, well, a pineapple. Frozen these three years in the youth fridge. Named by yours truly.

"We'll burn down the youth room," Davey replies. He doesn't say it in a distressed way. It's more of an FYI. Like he's maybe done something like this before. I'll light fire to that backstory eventually and smoke out some truth, but right now, it's all Bob, all the time.

The youth room microwave is from the eighties, black as coal, and built like a tank. No doubt donated by some senior church member who moved to assisted living. Its smell is a mix of baked beans, ramen noodles, and burnt popcorn (with the door closed). So if we properly execute bullet point number three (*Melt 50 Starlight Mints*), its condition will drastically improve.

Janie Lee laughs nervously, her UGGs bouncing against the wicker of the papasan. She's sipping hard on some vodka–wine cooler concoction Fifty has made. I give her a little fist-bump love for showing initiative. On both the rebellious drinking and the microwave. She doesn't offer me a drink. I don't need alcohol; I get drunk on schemes.

We begin.

The first three steps are disappointing. Pineapple Bob pops pretty loudly, as does the handful of Monopoly houses and hotels we've stolen from the game closet. The Starlight Mints have to be scraped off the microwave walls. It's more eventful when Mash pukes up wine cooler on a half-eaten bag of Twizzlers.

"Come on, man," Fifty says. "I wasn't done with those."

"You okay?" Janie Lee comforts Mash, which is pointless. Every group has a hurler: he is our hurler. He is used to puking. She is used to babying him. They are a very good team.

"Shhhhh with the upchucking," Woods orders.

Woods and I turn our attention to step four, which is seeing *How Many Peeps Is Too Many Peeps?* The answer: more than forty. It's messy and delightful.

Woods and I clean, reload, and move on to bullet five. Fifty moves on to more vodka. Typical. Step five involves boiling a used sock—Woods's, because he has the worst-smelling feet—in Dad's newly purchased *World's Best Preacher* mug. Two minutes in, we've got gym smell and no action. It's a little anti-climactic to be bullet five.

As we watch the mug-and-sock do its nothing, Woods says, "In basically three hours we have to be in the barn."

Fifty lifts his head from a plank position on the floor and says, "In three hours, we could be walking Vilmer's Beam." This makes Mash throw a blanket over his own head. Everyone is tired of hearing Fifty bellow about walking the loft beam in Vilmer's Barn. It was a dumb dare in fifth grade. We're seniors. We're over it.

I say, "I hate mornin—" and the sock catches on fire.

"Heck, *yeah!*" Mash says, too loud, and then laughs.

Janie Lee says, *"The other room!"* Because there is a group of our fellow youth snoozing in Youth Suite 202.

The fire is small—barely more than a magnifying-glass-on-grass sort of spark—and entirely worth the four steps that came before it.

"Hot cup of sock, good sir?" I ask in a British accent.

"Don't mind if I do," Woods says, reaching for the micro-wave door.

Davey sits bolt upright. "Do not—!"

The moment Woods opens the door, the small fire becomes a larger one. The mug rockets out of the microwave and explodes on the carpet. The fire—well, most of the fire—lands on a fuzzy blanket. The flames poof. Woods snatches the other sock—the one whose mate is now ablaze—and beats at the fire. He only fans the flames.

We are all screaming. There is more fire. More sparks. Both shoot out of the microwave; the antique appliance dismounts the counter and lands on the carpet with an explosive bang.

I imagine my father sitting up down the hall, scratching his head, lifting his nose toward the ceiling, sniffing. A yell gathers in his throat.

"Give me something to beat it out!" I shout, and Mash laughs so hard that he vomits again.

"Puke on the *fire*, man," Fifty says.

Davey shucks his jacket; Janie runs into the bathroom and returns with a damp towel. The jacket is working but not fast enough. Janie Lee throws the towel over the whole mess in a big Ta-da-I-will-fix-this fashion.

The fire is suddenly enormous.

"Was that the towel off the *floor*?" demands Woods as Davey rolls his eyes and says, "I'm calling 911."

Janie Lee shrinks from Woods's tone, nodding furiously. There's commotion in the hallway. The counter, where the microwave previously sat, is also on fire. The alarm begins a high-pitched wail and the sprinklers descend from the ceiling as if they are Jesus in the second coming. We are all getting soaked as Woods yells, "We used that towel to mop up *vodka*!"

It's hard to tell what is fire and what is smoke and what is microwave, but incredibly, I see the toe of the sock that started it all. Dad is going to kill me.

"Time to peace out," Davey says, gesturing toward the exit.

The fire alarm continues to pierce our eardrums. Woods throws open the door to the hallway. "Abandon ship!" he shouts gallantly. Always directing traffic. He's glistening with sweat. We all are, but he's glorying in it.

Mash throws last week's bulletin onto the fire before heading to the hallway. Fifty gives the wall a pound and yells, "Wakey, wakey. Church's on fire." Davey issues me a long look. He's got some *I told you so* in those eyes. I've got some *I know, I know* in mine.

I grab Janie Lee in her sweet pink sweatshirt and UGGs and drag her behind me into the hall. She's as soaked as the rest of us and not wearing a bra, and that's gonna be a problem when we hit cool autumn air.

I think: I didn't mean for *all this* to happen. I also think: I effing love Einstein the Whiteboard adventures. I have a moment of true fear when Woods plunges back inside the youth room. Before I even have time to process this, he reappears, coughing, and says, "Help me, Billie." He darts into the smoky room again.

In I go to rescue Woods, who wants to save his precious whiteboard. Einstein is too near the fire. The edge is already melted, and I assume too hot to touch. "I'll get you another one," I promise him.

Not what he wants to hear. I drag Woods away and shove him toward the back stairs.

Around us, kids are evacuating. They're carrying phones

and sleeping bags and pillow pets. Two sixth graders are getting on the elevators while Fifty screams at them, "Take the stairs! Didn't you learn anything in kindergarten?" A very familiar form is swimming upstream against the evacuees: Brother Scott McCaffrey. My tired and scared and angry father frantically counts everyone he sees. He flings opens doors, yells, moves to the next room. Precise words are impossible to hear over the fire alarm. But as I watch him check Youth Suite 201, I see he's putting two and two together.

Likely conclusion: where there's smoke, there's Billie.

Janie Lee and I quick-walk toward the exit. She pulls me against her and says right in my ear, so I hear it over the noise, "Billie, I think maybe I'm in love with Woods!"

"Jesus," I say, and hope it counts as a multipurpose prayer.

2

Fire trucks arrive at the curb—sirens blazing, ready to dispense water and large-coated men. Maybe the firefighters can put Dad out after they finish with the church. He's doing a roll call from his clipboard, blazing brighter than any flame we have made. Everyone is wet, amped, and accounted for. A couple of the junior high–ers are crying.

My crew has their butts on the asphalt, their backs against the church van. Janie Lee's pressed against me, and for once and only once I wish she'd give me space. She says, "I left my glasses in the bathroom."

"You'll get them back," I tell her, avoiding any form of eye contact.

Within twenty minutes, it's clear that the church will remain standing. But within those smoking, flaming, hosing minutes, the deacons have arrived. Hands are on hip replacements. Judgment is rampant. I overhear:

"Those youth can't be trusted."

"The preacher's daughter is the worst."

"I wonder if he'll do anything this time."

"He'll have to."

Dad walks purposefully toward the Hexagon, eyes blazing, knuckles white against the clipboard. He's about to crank it up and let us have it when his phone rings. The cell is ancient, has a ringer that rivals the fire alarm. He recognizes the number, and clearly expects whoever it is to yell at him about the fire. With a sigh and a warning look at us, he jams a finger in his ear and retreats.

"Uh-huh. Uh-huh. Say that again; I can't hear you. Oh, I see. Oh." Dad stops, his body stiffening. "I'm sorry. I'll have him call. Yes, him too."

He flips the phone closed—all the fight from his face morphed into sorrow. September in the South is still hot, but Dad shivers. He pinches the bridge of his nose and doesn't move. Woods grips my right elbow; Janie Lee leaves fingerprints on my left arm. Something worse than the church flambé has just happened.

He calls Mash and Davey over. A private conversation ensues that leaves them hugging and Mash indignant. "But Big T was just . . ." We watch Mash deflate like a balloon, words gone.

Dad gathers the rest of the group and explains the tragic

facts: Tyson Vilmer had a massive heart attack and ran off to meet the Lord while we were blowing up a sock. Without a word, with most everyone choking back tears, we link hands and say prayers of comfort for the Vilmer family.

My Grandy once said, *When that sweet old coot goes, he'll take all of Otters Holt with him.* I believed her then. I believe her now. Tyson Vilmer's life touched everyone who has ever lived and breathed Otters Holt air. A small-town butterfly effect.

Big T had one son, Harold, and one daughter, Hattie. Hattie moved away to Nashville, married, had Davey, separated, and just recently moved back in with her dad. Mash's parents have a better story. Harold went on a mission trip and fell in love with a black woman. There were no other interracial couples in Otters Holt, still aren't, but Tyson Vilmer walked his gorgeous daughter-in-law, Jeanelle, down the aisle and loved her like his own. That was eighteen years ago, and the first wedding my dad ever officiated. Jeanelle has since been awarded a Corn Dolly, 2012. It doesn't sound like much to the rest of the world, but that was groundbreaking for Otters Holt.

I call Grandy. She is awake, voice cloudy and broken. Someone on the telephone chain reached her first. "Dad just told us about Big T," I say. She's crying the way old people do, reserved, composed. She's the type to use a Kleenex or a handkerchief instead of her sleeve. I say, "I just wanted to tell you I love you." We hang up so I can check on Davey and she can bake a casserole for the Vilmer family.

"This blows." Fifty's bluntness is appropriate for once.

Janie Lee and Woods automatically take their places at Mash's side. We've done death before. My granddad. Fifty's aunt. Woods's mom lost a baby five years ago. We've learned how to huddle up like a football team to tackle the shit out of grief.

I leech myself to Davey without actually touching him. I tell him I'm incredibly sorry about Big T. I also admit *sorry* is a lackluster word. We stare at a nub of moon, him presumably thinking of Big T, me thinking of Big T and everything else. This night. The fire. The ramifications. Janie Lee's impromptu confession. The *ramifications*. Emotions lap me, round and round.

I stop thinking because Janie Lee scoots next to me. "I saw Big T yesterday. He gave me a peppermint."

"Me too," Woods says, joining us.

Mash says, "He loved peppermints," even though we know.

After Dad handles the immediate red tape with the deacons and fire chief, we trudge mournfully to the church van and Dad drives toward the Vilmer farm in near silence. Day-old McDonald's and smoke smells become our burden to bear for the next ten minutes.

I'm sidesaddling the captain's seat across from Dad. He's wearing the blank expression of prayer. Poor Mash has his head on Janie Lee's flannel lap; her fingers weave and love their way around his ears and scalp and braids. Davey has the whole back row. He's texting someone. Mash spent the first years of his life riding on his granddad's shoulders. I wonder where Davey fits

into that equation. Fifty sobers up in the middle, and Woods—
Woods tries to decide whether he can tell a story yet. I know
this because our telepathy isn't all that miraculous. His eyes
are the windows of his brain. I nod, agreeing that it's appropriate to speak.

"You know . . ." Woods begins. He tells four, maybe five,
tales about Tyson Vilmer while Dad navigates the curves on
Stoney Temple Road. Stories we all know. Woods is one of
those people who make you hang on their recycled words. By
the end of his yarns, Mash is sitting upright, adding details,
Dad has stopped sucking air through his front teeth, and
Janie Lee touches Woods's shoulder in thanks. Her hand lingers there for a three count and lands on my elbow, sticking
like glue. Davey's still texting, still glazed, still apart. Fifty's
asleep.

And as I look out over my Hexagon . . . I'm . . . well, I'm in
love with them all. Death can muddle beliefs and raise questions, but it makes love crystal clear.

We roll into Mash's driveway at four thirty a.m., because
that's where the family has gathered. Already cars and trucks
are parked willy-nilly. Church members march antlike in and
out of the farmhouse wearing red-rimmed eyes and ratty
robes, delivering frozen casseroles—prepared for occasions
like this—and promises of support. Each person bows in
tearful sympathy as Mash and Davey make their way to the
screen door. Mash's back hitches with a deep breath. He goes
inside. We all follow and take our turns sorrying the Vilmers

and mustering brave faces. Janie Lee, Woods, Fifty, and I park ourselves in Mash's room and poke each other to stay awake, unsure of what Davey and Mash might need upon return from the living room. The boys arrive an hour later, noses running, saying their parents said we should all try and rest. The first rays of pink morning light peek through the mini-blinds like a watercolor painting streaking the hardwood.

"Thanks for staying," Mash says.

But he knows there is nowhere else we'd rather be.

We fall asleep in a big pile on the floor. When I wake around noon, I'm Woods's little spoon and Janie Lee's big spoon. Mash and Davey are back-to-back and snoring heavily. Fifty has moved to the bed. I have to pee, but I hold it for an hour, not wanting to wake anyone else. For most of that hour, I cry and chat with God on three grievances: death, forgiveness, and jealousy. Prayer is my live journal. It's the one place I don't ever have to be a rock star about life. I figure if God made my tear ducts, He has to deal with me using them. I wrap up with a final promise. "And if you could help me with the Janie Lee problem and the church fire, I'll never get that stupid with Einstein again."

When everyone is awake, we take turns going home to change our smoky pajamas and shower off last night's crazy.

By luck, Janie Lee and I return to Mash's driveway at the same time. She's replaced the lost bra and looks surprisingly sexy in sweats. I can tell she's gotten ready in a hurry. No jewelry. No makeup. She was probably trying to run out the door before her mom could task her with hours at Bleach, the coin Laundromat they manage.

"You tell your mom about the fire?" I ask, expecting a no. It's not that the Millers aren't understanding people; it's that, well, setting a church ablaze is just the sort of thing one would expect from a Miller. Her dad has been in and out of jail, her mom has a reputation for selling powders that aren't of the washing variety, and her brother got a one-way ticket to the military, courtesy of Judge Cox.

But she nods. "Oh, she already knew. Heard it from Conner, who heard it from Johnny, who heard it from his aunt Miriam."

Unsurprising. I'm sure people picked up their phones last night and opened conversations with, "I just called to let you know Tyson Vilmer died," and closed with, "Did you hear Community Church had a fire in the youth room?" And they likely had additional commentary.

"She angry?" I ask.

"She's the usual. Eleven months, B. Eleven more months."

The usual means Mrs. Miller wants to know how much it will cost and if it will affect "the family business." Eleven months is the amount of time until Janie Lee cracks all the rearview mirrors when she blows out of Otters Holt.

She's been keeping a countdown since before she could count.

Janie Lee and I have many similarities: A love of art and music. BBC shows and reruns of anything with Betty

White. Neither of us is scared of spiders, and we both love the incessant humming of cicadas in a plague year. She'd kill a whole day lying beside me in the grass, face up to the sky, sun beaming down. But Janie Lee will not be lying in that tall bluegrass eleven months from now, because she does not share my love of our hometown. While I say, "I'm from Otters Holt," she says, "I'm from Western Kentucky." That's as proud as she gets.

Janie Lee pulls me into the mother of all side hugs. She smells much better than the last time she side-hugged me.

"I'll fix this church stuff. Somehow," I tell her.

She believes me and says, "Last night seems like a million years ago."

Two million.

She starts to say something else, but Davey reappears in a very non–Otters Holt, very new, and very shiny black Audi R8. Whoever is driving doesn't get out or put the car in park. Davey slinks from the passenger side, eyeliner reapplied, one crumpled band shirt swapped out for the next. We wait on him to saunter over before we head to Mash's room. Neither of us asks after the Audi, but I'm dying to. Sweet ride of Satan, it's beautiful.

Fifty's practically licking the windowpane when we all get inside. "Nice wheels."

Davey coughs up a name. "Thomas."

"Thomas," Fifty mouths behind Davey's back. He puckers his lips and makes a kissing noise.

Huh, maybe, I think. They could be a thing. Then again, Fifty thinks everyone will bag anyone.

Woods removes his fingers from the mini-blinds. Steps away from the window and falls on Mash's bed. "Five things to do with an Audi," he says in his rule-the-world way.

"Five things to do *in* an Audi," Fifty corrects.

"Ah, Einstein," Janie Lee says nostalgically.

"He'll rise again." Woods's imperial face says, *After the funeral, people, after the funeral.*

Fifty claps Mash on the shoulder and pushes him sideways onto the bed. Fifty has four older brothers. Shoving people around is his love language. Except then he adds, "You know, I hate to say it, but your granddad dying saved our ass."

We stare slack-jawed at Fifty.

"*What?*" Fifty says. "You're all thinking it too."

Nope. I'm thinking: *Big T was an adult I genuinely liked.* I'm thinking: *He's always held off the wolves from Brother Scott McCaffrey and his wayward daughter. With Tyson alive, this fire thing would have been a nonissue.* I'm thinking: *With Tyson dead, Dad could face serious consequences from my actions. Again.*

Woods tells Fifty to shut it so no one else has to, and Fifty is maybe red-cheeked, but it's hard to tell with all that facial hair. "I'm not glad he's dead," he corrects. "Mash knows that."

He shoves Mash again. Mash shoves back. They're fine.

Davey drops his phone in the back pocket of his jeans, rejoins the conversation. "Oh, we know what you meant." It comes out more like, *We know who you are.*

Davey's texting habits distract me. Was his last text—the one right before he stowed his phone—to Audi Thomas? Is that who Davey texts when the rest of us don't need to text anyone because we are all there? He must have a whole group of friends back in Nashville. They must love him in a way we're only scratching at, and I wonder if it's lonely to be with us instead of them.

For the rest of the day, we distract Mash and Davey with cards, food, and more Best of Tyson Vilmer stories. The time he played Wiffle ball, put a pie in Tawny Jacobs's face, rode Mash on the tractor, gave the library all his books. The time he did everything and anything needed. We even drive to the edge of town and try to sit mournfully beneath the Molly the Corn Dolly statue. Frankly, it's difficult to sit mournfully beside a forty-foot-tall blazing-yellow roadside attraction. So we play a few rounds of Hacky Sack and brag to intermittent tourists that Mash and Davey's granddad is the one who built Molly the Corn Dolly. The tourists seem suitably impressed.

In late afternoon, we're back in Mash's room when Jeanelle leans through the doorway. There's a poker game and a box of chicken in the center of our circle. We quiet down. "If you're willing"—she dabs her eyes with a Kleenex—"Harold would appreciate you helping out with the funeral. Big T wrote down what he wanted in the King James. You're all a part."

There are two things every old person in Otters Holt has: a King James with "arrangements" and a list of Corn Dolly winners taped to the fridge.

Jeanelle shifts a deep-pink hair wrap and gathers her thoughts. Even now, when she is so clearly sad, she wears a touch of pink eye shadow that makes her face look thirty instead of forty.

She starts assigning tasks. "Janie Lee and Woods, will you do your thing?"

Their thing is a musical combo: violin, and piano and vocals. They've been performing together since Janie Lee picked up a bow in fourth grade. I hate them a little when they play. I can sing; they bend notes to their whims and instruments to their wants.

"He has the rest of you as pallbearers," Jeanelle tells us.

We nod, as if this is expected.

We do the other expected things too. Visitation. Sad hearts. More sleeping piles.

The morning of the funeral, I shower at my house and ask Mom about dress codes. I've been to dozens of funerals—a terrible by-product of having a minister as a father. They are the one time I venture into the recesses of my closet and emerge with one of the two black dresses I own. But today, I'm thinking black pants are the ticket.

"I can wear this?" I point to the clothes laid out on my bed. I'm still walking softly because of the fire.

Mom fastens pearls behind her neck and checks her nail polish after the clasping. That leaves her to survey my room.

"Yes to the clothes. No to your boots. And please move this stuff to the garage before your dad comes back here."

My room is totally undone. A half-carved wooden elephant head is on my desk. Eight canvases lean in the corner. Another four are on the floor. The paints and dirty brown cup of water are out too. They're from Thursday night. A whirlwind of clothes from this weekend's comings and goings threatens to swallow the clothes I've laid out.

I'm not trying to be an asshole, but I'm wearing the boots.

The Audi is in the parking lot when I get out of my parents' minivan at the funeral home. While I'm staring, the car produces Thomas and Davey from its small bowels. Audi Thomas is black—a notable feature in our lily-white-except-for-Mash-and-Jeanelle town—and built like one of those guys who drinks three too many protein shakes a day. He also has the confident stride of someone who has all his daddy's credit cards in his wallet. Davey's lanky and lean beside him. They walk into the funeral home wearing identical suits and ties except for the difference between navy and steel gray.

Even from behind, Davey appears changed. Back straight as a ruler. Hands buried in his pockets like a politician's son. His shoes are high gloss.

Inside, Hattie pins a white rose to Davey's suit coat and then pins one to my shirt. I find my place among the other pallbearers. Mom clarified this morning that I was an honorary pallbearer—"Girls do not carry caskets," she had said. Honorary my ass. I stand with Davey, Thomas, Mash, Fifty, and three other men from church, hoping all these guys ate their Wheaties, because Tyson Vilmer was a Great Pyrenees of a man. When you pick up a casket, you feel the weight of it very differently than you think you will. We carry it. It carries us. The real weight is carrying each other.

Death is a superhuman burden.

When Tyson Vilmer is front and center, where he belongs, all the pallbearers but me sit in a reserved section. I slide in next to Grandy. Her velvet hand with its spidery blue veins lands in mine. I let her cling. I even cling back when Woods and Janie Lee shred the entire funeral home with "A Satisfied Mind" followed by "How Great Thou Art."

Then Dad shreds it with his eulogy. A good thing because of the conversation I had with Janie Lee this morning:

"You see the paper?" she asked.

I hadn't.

"There was a full page about Big T and . . ." She drew a banner with her hand. "'Community Church Aflame,'" followed by a big fat pause.

"'Community Church Aflame' and . . ."

"And . . . 'Local Minister Sleeps Through Blaze.'"

I'm vexed. "That's not even true."

Truth hardly played a part in the local news.

Now Dad's telling a story about the Harvest Festival, and how without Tyson's support this will likely be its last year. Our spines bend like dying flowers. The congregation responds. Grief knocks into grief. No one can imagine Otters Holt without the Harvest Festival. Without Tyson. Least of all my tear-streaked father.

I look away from him and notice three things. A) Janie Lee has her pinkie on Woods's knee; B) Davey has his head on Thomas's big-ass Thor shoulder; and C) there's a muscular man looking like Davey will in thirty years, who is practically sitting on top of Davey's mom. She is not sad; she's furious.

And then I manhandle the casket to the car and the casket to the earth and say my final good-bye. "Thank you, you sweet old coot." *Tyson Vilmer. b. 1938.—d. 2017. Beloved by Otters Holt.* (Not the official inscription, but I'm close.)

Dad catches my eye, narrows his expression. *I still remember that you blew up the youth room.*

No worries, Brother Scott. So do I.

3

Dad in his ratty bathrobe, unshaven at two in the afternoon. Dad alone in his study, Bible open, heart closed, at two in the morning. Dad gazing and blazing at the newspaper article. For one week, I leave him to his heartache, aware that I am a contributing factor.

I was grounded before the fire. For attitude, back-talking, and breaking Dad's *Coolest Minister Ever* mug. The weekend of the fire I was interrogated. I explained about the sock, I admitted to the vodka; I bore the weight of responsibility. "It was my idea and my alcohol," I told Mom and Dad apologetically. Mom yelled herself hoarse. Dad walked away. She was fine in a day. He was . . . well, since then we've had a baker's dozen of passive-aggressive interactions and only one real conversation.

My goal was to apologize, genuinely. Which I did. But the

end result was us screaming about my "inability to understand my position in this family."

Oh, I understand my position quite well. "Brother Scott McCaffrey demands perfection," I say.

Our words are between a snarl and a growl. I shut him in his home office with a door slam that rattles the frame. Through the wood, he yells, "Not perfection. Effort. Where is your effort?"

He makes me old just listening to him.

Dad has a common problem among ministers: he reproduced.

While our argument is exacerbated by the fire, most of our "discussions" are of the agree-to-disagree variety. Somewhere, buried under all this angst, hardwired in, we have a sturdy core. I am his baby girl and he is my big strong father. I love him even when I hate him. Like . . . if I close my eyes on any given summer day, I feel him lift me into an azure sky—a basketball falls through a hoop, he cheers. There's the denim of his Wranglers on my bare legs as I drive a pickup on my tenth birthday. The cotton of his T-shirt as we piggyback down Grandy's steps Christmas morning. The two of us stand at the observation point at Niagara Falls—Mom is sketching in the grass—and he tells me, "Baby, you can be anyone."

The positive-memory well stops around the time I turned thirteen. We exchanged memories for yells, trust for suspicion, ease for tension. According to him, I'm my mother's daughter. She was the art major, a Canadian liberal. Back before monogrammed shirts and the Lord, my mom was a real shit-starter.

I think about her. How she handles him. I nudge open his office door and give him another shot. "I meant what I said. We never meant for anything bad to happen."

"Billie . . . I believe you. But the problem is . . ."

"No one else does."

His chin drops in defeat.

There's really nothing more to say. Back in the garage, I let myself get snagged in a project I've been working on for months. I call it the Daily Sit—a (someday) fully functional couch made mostly of old newspapers and glue. I'm busy adding another layer of epoxy when Davey pulls into my driveway and wheels his fancy-schmancy Camaro all the way up to where I'm working.

He's dressed as usual: navy bandanna headband pushing his hair skyward, black skinny-ish jeans, lace-up high-tops, and a white T-shirt he's cut the sleeves from even though it's sixty-five degrees. I'm dressed like I've been in the garage all day. He assesses both the Daily Sit and me. Seems interested.

"Mom has me out delivering thank-you packages," he says. I've got newsprint and glue up to my elbows, so he tosses something wrapped in craft paper on the workbench.

"For what?" I ask.

He mounts our chest freezer and slaps his high-tops against the side. "Being a pallbearer for Big T. So, was that weird for you?"

I don't look. One ornery corner of the newsprint is curling up like a cat's tail. "No," I say, realizing I've glued two fingers to the armrest. I jerk them away and cuss.

Davey's too busy checking out my workspace to care about my loss of skin. The garage is both oddly organized and incredibly chaotic. There's Guinevere, a lady knight constructed of aluminum cans, two prototypes of a book television I built for Woods, stacks of newspaper for the Daily Sit, a half dozen semi-constructed metal unicorns near my welding bench, and supplies most people would call trash.

"You do all this?" he asks.

I can't tell if he's impressed or trying to work out why I haven't finished anything. "Yeah," I admit. "Everyone needs a hobby."

"Especially in a town like this."

"Oh, don't be so judgmental. Otters Holt inspires imagination that big cities don't."

"I wasn't being judgmental," he says.

"You were, but I'll give you a pass for now."

I opt to join him on the freezer, thinking I'll add another layer to the Daily Sit tomorrow after church. "Some of us have to make our own fun."

"I make my own fun."

There's something sly and opaque behind his expression that tells me we are not opposites, which had been my theory until Big T died. Until then, I assumed he was in Otters Holt because he had to be and in the Hexagon because of Mash. He didn't seem lonely; he seemed both cultivated and uncertain, always hesitating. The way I was as a kid.

I dip my shoulder into his and tease him out. "I'm not sure you even know how to spell the word *fun*."

His chin lodges against his breastbone. His feet stop swinging. "I didn't know you were keeping up with me."

I tell him the truth. "I keep up with everything."

Davey's got potential—the movement, the thrill, is all there. It's hidden, but when Davey smiles, really smiles, the dictionary doesn't have an adequate word for the effect. It's fully charged, alive. I want to give him a reason to do it again.

Quite unexpectedly, he asks, "How would you like to keep up with me this evening?"

I make a show of dusting my hands as if the work in the garage is all done forever. "Sure. What's the occasion?"

"Change of scenery. Costume party in Nashville?"

Well, damn. No rigidity to that. I'm overjoyed to hear that his grief is moving nicely along the normal healing continuum. I've noticed Mash has been able to reference his granddad without burrowing inside his T-shirt this past week. And over the past few days, Davey was able to say "died" and "Big T" without stuttering. The rest of us stopped trading shifts at their houses. Which is good; I've had about all the barbecue sandwiches and red velvet cake I can manage. Another thing I can't manage: Janie Lee scooting close to Woods on the hardwood floor of Mash's bedroom. So Davey's suggestion, a change of scenery, feels downright hopeful.

"Will Audi Thomas be at this costume party?"

He grins. "Indeed."

"Indeed," I repeat.

I need to clean up and get permission. Before Davey knows it, he agrees to add another layer of newsprint to the Daily Sit while he waits. I instruct him to make that ornery flap his obedient servant.

Inside, I address the parents. "Davey's here. We're gonna run around if it's okay with you?" I focus on Mom instead of Dad, and of course, get opposing answers.

"Yes," says Mom. "No," says Dad.

In a heartbeat, this is their argument, not mine. "Honey, united front," Dad demands.

"Oh, unite your own front," she says without any malice. "He just lost his granddad."

Other than funeral friend watch, I've barely ventured from the garage, assuming "out of sight, out of mind" is a good strategy. Although all this time in my workshop gave me plenty of time to stew over the possibility of Woods and Janie Lee coupling up, which only turned into me making terrible paintings of two-headed unicorns and having awful dreams where everyone I know and love claims they hate me. I don't know which part irks me worst: her liking him or him possibly liking her back. I probably need this trip as badly as Davey does.

"Please," I say to my parents, greasing the wheel. "I'd really like to go."

Whether Dad remembers that I'm not evil or that Davey is

probably in need of company, the pushback ends. I skate trium-
phantly from the room and shower off nearly eighty percent of
the glue. Win-win. I settle on a costume, make the necessary
transformation, and toss a change of regular clothes in a duffel.

When I sneak my costume past the parents—they would
not approve of cross-dressing—it takes Davey a moment to
realize I'm dressed as him. My hair, which is the same color
as his—a dark brown that is almost black and nearly the same
length—is parted, glued (thanks to Janie Lee's stash of cosmet-
ics in my bathroom), and bandanna-ed to mirror his style. It
isn't hard to emulate his clothes: scissors to every piece of fabric on my body. I added silver accessories. I added sideburns.
Because I am an overachiever, I added makeup that angles
my chin, triples my eyebrows, and hints at an Adam's apple.
Though that part is flubbed.

"That's sort of hilarious," he says, circling me.

I'm pleased he's pleased.

He continues his survey. I get the feeling he's not looking at
my clothes, but somewhere deeper. He says, "I thought you'd
fit in with my cosplay friends." He means, *I thought you'd fit in
with me.* And I finally feel like I'm getting somewhere with this
boy.

"Cause-what?" I ask.

"Cosplay."

"Is that like chains and whips?" I am not balking just yet,
but perhaps I have underestimated him.

Davey laughs in earnest, head back, teeth showing. "No. A

cosplay party is just a regular old costume party that doesn't use Halloween as an excuse to dress up."

"What are you going as?" I ask.

"Good question. They just called, so I'm going to throw something together." He uses the utility sink to clean his arms and then paws around in the trunk of his car. He comes up with a navy V-neck sweater, tie, and white dress shirt. After shucking his T-shirt and tossing it onto the Daily Sit, he eyeballs the knight in the corner while he dresses and expertly ties a Windsor. He asks if the knight has a name. Certainly. I name everything. "Guinevere," I say.

"Is she stable enough to borrow?"

If he wants to borrow a half-assembled lady knight, who am I to stop him? We toss Guinevere in among the thank-you gifts, and I toss myself among the books on his front seat. Graphic novels. A biography on Teddy Roosevelt. *Sex for Dummies.* One of those cheap sketchbooks from the bargain aisle.

"Doing some extracurricular reading?" I ask, and drop the books on the back floorboard.

"Roosevelt, yes. Sex, no. That's Mash's copy. Comic, hell yeah and always."

You gotta love a guy who throws his cousin under the sexually inexperienced bus.

I'm pretty enamored with Davey's car. The seats are leather, the radio is exquisite—like the bands are playing in my lap—and he's got another tie hanging from the rearview mirror. Did I mention it's a V-8 engine with 455 thoroughbreds under the hood and a manual transmission? Did I mention I drive a bicycle?

I give the tie a swing—it's identical to the one he's wearing. "This from your last school?"

"My last life." He shifts, revs, off we go. "You want me to dress as you?" he asks when we hit the interstate.

No. Yes. It would be funny. "I'd like to see you try."

I am glad we're joking. Since he moved to Otters Holt, he's been dawdling through the school hallways, chin always down, moving the way this one Death Cab for Cutie song sounds. Trudge. Trudge. Sad. Sad.

Davey drives a little bit like he behaves: erratic, but safe. He doesn't listen to a single band I've ever heard of.

"Tell me about where we're going," I say.

He counters. "Tell me about Woods."

I turn down the music. "I can talk eloquently about pine, oaks, sometimes birch. They're harder. I confuse them with sycamores."

He flicks my thigh.

"What do you want to know?" I ask.

"Everything."

I tell him *everything* he's missed in the last seventeen years. Stunts, history, fake weddings, other items we've set on fire. Forty minutes later, he says, "You didn't say the real thing."

I raise my sunglasses. "Which is?"

"You've got some serious attraction going on." He's fishing, but he's nearly sure of himself.

I can't give myself away. "Maybe I don't."

He pokes the bear. "Maybe you're a liar?"

The bear pokes back. "Maybe I never lie."

"Maybe you only lie to yourself."

I guess while I was studying him, he was studying me. I turn the radio back to full blast until Batman is in the sky in Nashville. (The Batman Building: that's what Davey calls the skyscraper that looks like a superhero.) The Cumberland River snakes beneath lit bridges through downtown. Traffic sucks. I roll the window down and listen to the sheer noise of the city: cars, horns, sirens, construction.

"Things at church going to be okay?" he asks when he passes a fire truck.

"They're bleak," I tell Davey.

"You feel guilty."

He's not asking, so I don't bother nodding. I don't destroy things; I repurpose them. Even tiny little things that other people throw out—paper clips and pennies and confetti. So I would never destroy a church on purpose. The church is a symbol of faith, Jesus, my principles. I don't pretend that trio works for everyone, but I never ever meant to crap where I eat.

If I'd known what the fallout would be for Dad—the newspaper, the subsequent deacon meetings, the anger—I'd have erased Einstein.

We arrive outside a coffee shop east of the river, and Davey explains what we're about to do. Essentially, we're joining a "private" club—a contingent of acquaintances from two schools: one all-girls, one all-boys. From his description, I determine that this academy of his is either the Hogwarts of Nashville or a rip-off *Dead Poets Society*. I also determine that his father must be filthy rich and that Otters Holt is a few notches down the economic ladder. Hello, modified Camaro. Hello, rich-people activities like raising cheetahs or some crazy shit like that. Hello, Davey's friends.

The Audi is in the parking lot.

"Audi Thomas," I say.

"You plan to call him that?"

"Well, yeah. I don't know anyone else who drives an Audi."

"You don't know any other Thomases."

"I'm still going to call him Audi Thomas."

"I wouldn't. He hates that car."

"No one in their right mind hates a black, gorgeous thing that goes zero to sixty in four seconds." I looked up the specs the weekend of the funeral. Price too. New: $162,900.

"Okay, Thomas hates when people make assumptions about him based on the car."

"Audi Thomas," I correct, unwilling to bend. "If you own a car that costs more than the church parsonage, that car goes before your name."

Despite, or perhaps because of, my insults, Davey says, "He's going to like you a lot."

"We carried a casket together. We already bonded."

The casket comment lands like a plane with a flat front

tire. He breathes, I breathe, we skip ahead to who else will be in attendance. Davey reels off a list and concludes with, "Plus, Gerry. She's your people for sure."

My people. It'll be interesting to crosscheck his perceptions.

I don't have to wait. A girl clad in leather, fishnets, boots similar to mine, and a generous portion of sexy smacks the hood and growls at us. "Gerry," Davey says.

Gerry opens the driver's side door, and Davey slides his seat back. A good choice, because she hurls herself sideways onto his lap, loosens his tie, and says, "Holy hell, David Winters, I've missed you. When are you moving home?"

Then she puts her lips to his lips with a big *mwah.* She's *my* people? Holy hell, indeed.

Gerry has hair the color of the Green Goblin, and if it's spray-in, it's damn convincing. I'm guessing she cut it herself . . . with kindergarten scissors. There's a quirky upside-down-triangle tattoo behind her ear and six piercings in her cartilage. I barely have time to count them because she says, "Your turn, David's friend." She tugs my shirt, and we're ChapStick to ChapStick. It's not just a *mwah.* I have time to think *I'm kissing a girl. I've never kissed a girl before.*

So here's a surprise: I kiss her back. Because . . . well, she's so present. So alive. So magnanimous. And when she is kissing me, all the death of the last week disappears.

"Hi," I say, and wipe my tingling lips.

"Oh, I like her." Gerry pops Davey on the arm. "Your girl passes the test."

I'd like to see what happens when she meets Janie Lee. If Janie Lee also "passes the test."

Davey twists his smile sideways and arches an eyebrow. "One of these days you're going to get socked."

She doesn't disagree. She checks me out, lingers on my boots, and then she says to Davey, "You said she was beautiful, but you didn't say she was hot."

Gerry's words catch me woefully off guard. Beautiful? Hot? I've been called many things. Among them dyke and bulldagger (when my hair was very, very short), tomboy, and hoyden (that's a favorite of the volleyball team). Someone once asked me if I was trying to be Angelina Jolie in her Billy Bob Thornton years. I still have no idea what that means, but it doesn't sound good. Right now, I'm dressed as a dude. So there's that.

"Thank you," I manage.

"This fluid thing you have going is a thing of substance." She smiles at me. Her mouth opens so wide I could stuff an entire state in there.

I don't know her well enough to make a tombstone, but I do it anyway. The perks of having your tongue in a stranger's mouth. *Gerry. b. ?—d. probably never. Here Lies Gerry: People followed her to Mars.* Tombstones aren't about death. They're about legacy. I shouldn't care what people think, but it's hard to avoid that someone else gets the last word. I try to live in such a way that I predetermine those words. I get the sneaky suspicion that Gerry does too.

"Also, your hair *is* longer, Davey," she tells him as if he has not looked in a mirror since he moved.

"Like it?"

"Like it? I love it. It's a very struck-by-lightning motif you've got going."

Perhaps he wants to say more, but we all turn our attention to the characters gathering in the parking lot. Gerry and I help Davey into Guinevere, which makes him clank like cans behind a wedding car. (Guinevere had been one of my art disappointments until now.) Gerry applies makeup to Davey's face while I adjust the suspenders holding Guinevere in place. For good sport, I let Gerry attack my face as well. The powder smell makes me gag, the additional eyeliner tickles my lids, but I like the way she clips my hair in the exact same way she has clipped Davey's. Twinsies.

We're not known characters, but we're characters all the same.

Audi Thomas arrives on the scene. He's dressed as a mash-up of Han Solo and Chewie. Our formal meeting goes something like this:

"You're Billie."

"You're Audi Thomas?"

Fake scowl. "You burned down a church."

"You should burn down that outfit."

"Says the girl dressed like David."

Gerry butts in. "I kissed her."

"You kiss everyone."

Audi Thomas and Gerry share a peck.

Audi Thomas offers to marry me. I ask for a rain check. Everyone laughs. We all go inside. Understated conclusion of the year: I am not in Otters Holt anymore.

We stroll into a coffee shop whose patrons are part Marvel Universe, part J. J. Abrams, part anime with a sprinkle of Disney. Even in costumes, some very elaborate, Thomas recognizes everyone. There are a few "normal" prep students in chinos and dress shirts. He knows them too. The barista is Johnny. Johnny lifts a large mug in the air and yells, "Americano, David? Thomas?"

Davey asks what I want. No clue. We don't have coffee shops in Otters Holt, so I suggest that he rich-pick me something. He claims he's not rich. I claim he has purchased enough five-dollar drinks that Johnny the Barista knows his order by heart. And then to make a point, I tap a large, square, expensive-looking ring on his finger. I win.

Davey lifts two digits in the air, and Johnny gives him a thumbs-up. Davey knows how to coffee shop, and I attempt to adopt his comfort. After twenty straight minutes of playing the meeting game, I ask, "How come you don't know everyone?"

He sips his Americano, hiding behind the mug. "Thom's branched out since I moved."

We—Thomas, Gerry, Davey, and I—have been a comfortable, revolving foursome. I'm not saying we would dog pile now, but I think we might dog pile before the night is over. Here, Davey's a watercolor with smeared edges and paint running down the page. Loose. At home, he's a pencil draw-ing. I like this Davey better.

"What's with all the formality?" I ask, after Thomas calls him David for the third time tonight.

"Davey's a Vilmer family thing," he explains.

Thomas kicks his head back, grins wickedly, eyes gleaming with something more than laughter. "His old man wouldn't let us call him Davey."

"Not in a million years," Davey agrees.

The two of them sound drunk on caffeine. I can't blame them. The Americano spiked my pulse too. That doesn't stop them from wanting round two. Thomas and Davey steal away to the coffee bar for Johnny's miracle brew, which leaves me with Gerry, who is readjusting the hoop in her nose. She's older than I am. Maybe nineteen or twenty. From all her stories, she is a vagabond wrapped in a mystery inside a costume. There are unasked questions hanging off her lips.

I beat her to the punch. "Do you really kiss everyone you meet?"

"Will you sell me those boots?" she asks in return.

I'm on one barstool. My boots are propped high on another. I swivel and place one foot on each of her thighs so she can see what she's missing in the boot department. "I would sell you my beating heart before I'd sell these boots. Now, the kissing. Explain."

Gerry chews the nail of her pinkie—eats some of the scant black polish. "I don't kiss everyone. I kiss the people who have

49

the little pieces of my soul I've been looking for."

Gerry's explanation makes a degree of sense. My soul has always felt like a big game of Where's Waldo? Most days I go about life and see no signs of a red-and-white cap. But sometimes, there among the ordinary, I discover misplaced pieces of self. She's saying she's one of them. Honestly, it's a relief to know that pieces exist beyond the Hexagon. Without safe people, I would climb a tree and never come down.

I'd tell Gerry that she's my people, but if I had to say it aloud, she wouldn't be.

"Please say you're coming back for LaserCon?"

"Should I?" I ask, without having a clue what LaserCon is.

"In my opinion, everyone should. But I'm guessing David could use your company. His granddad's death hit him pretty hard."

It's difficult to hear about Davey's emotional health from someone who exists outside of Otters Holt. All those outgoing text messages. This means Davey is hiding in old sanctuaries rather than leaning into the Hexagon. I glance over my shoulder at him. He's demonstrating a leprechaun-looking toe-tap for Johnny and Audi Thomas. All of the recent tension in his shoulders has relaxed, and he's clanking like a proper aluminum Guinevere should. He's electric.

Then it hits me: Davey Winters is in love.

He's got Audi Thomas graffitied all over his face. Thom may very well be with Gerry, but long before there was Gerry, there was something with Davey.

No wonder he's been so tentative with the Hexagon. His mom didn't move him from Nashville to Otters Holt; she moved him from love to absence.

The timing of this realization coincides with the band taking the stage. Everywhere in Nashville is a live music venue. The Ryman plus the Grand Ole Opry plus a rinky-dink coffee shop filled with rich high school kids. The drummer pounds her sticks—"One, two, three"—and the leader, a punk girl Davey says goes to their sister school, puts a lung into the mic.

We are invited to set down our coffees and power up our feet.

As soon as Davey shucks Guinevere, he tugs me by the index finger to the middle of the dance floor, Gerry and Audi Thomas on our heels. Those two lean and lean and lean until their foreheads touch. Gerry collects another piece of her soul from Audi Thomas's mouth. We watch them for a moment, waiting for a dance style to emerge. Just after the stillness, they jump.

We all jump.

Just like that, my heartbeat is a kick drum. My hands punch the air. Davey and I leap like we're on a trampoline. *Spring. Spro-ing. Spring.* With total abandon. From our neck movements to our toes striking the polished concrete, we're timed perfectly. My god, his eyelashes are long. We land on each other's feet. We hurl ourselves toward the ceiling.

Around us, everyone I've met, from Captain America to Princess Jasmine, lets go of something they've been holding on to.

For me, it's the fire. Up. Down. It's Janie Lee's confession. Up. Down. It's my fucking inability to finish the projects in my garage. Up. Down. It's my father. Up. Down. It's expectations. Up. Down. It's self-acceptance. Up. Down.

I pray a hard-rock, punk, dancing, live-journal prayer.

Here I am. Free me.

There he is. Free Davey.

There they all are. Free everyone.

We're jumping to the words "I can't be contained."

In the middle of everyone else leaping and screaming, I stand completely still and fully embrace the eye of the cosplay hurricane. The power of so many people doing the same thing rushes through my veins like blood. From the costumes to the dancing, we're caught up in the same palm of an invisible hand.

I am dressed as a boy, I have kissed a girl, I have met people outside my usual web. No one cares. I am hidden. I am perfectly transparent.

This is it. This is living.

Davey lands. His feet plant. Sweat drips down the sides of his face, making lines in his makeup that look like a cracked desert floor. "You're smiling so loudly I heard it over the music," he says.

I think of kissing him the way Gerry kissed me. But Thomas . . . But Woods.

Instead, we jump like fools until Johnny tells us it's closing time.

4

We're homeward bound, discussing my Dance Dance Revelation, when I eyeball the clock: 10:45. "Can you speed up?" I ask, and monkey over the console to change clothes in the backseat.

Dammit. I didn't bring makeup remover. Not only am I cutting it close on curfew, I'm arriving with sideburns. As it turns out, freedom is a temporary thing found only in coffee shops in other cities.

"What's the problem there?" Davey asks at my sudden disappearance.

I wiggle out of slashed jeans and into sweatpants. "His name is Brother Scott McCaffrey."

"Oh, right." Having been in Otters Holt for three months, Davey is not an expert on his youth minister. But that *oh* rings of understanding. "What's your take on things?"

I scrub at my face with the discarded T-shirt. "You mean God?"

"No. I'm good with God. I only mean . . . church people seem awfully hard on you for you to keep loving them."

Church people. Trite. I level a glare at him in the rearview. Davey cracks open a window. Then cracks the one beside me. The glue in my hair holds. I won't be able to fix it before I see Dad.

Davey speaks. "You seemed pretty happy, pretty uninhibited tonight. And don't get me wrong, you're usually happy enough, but I always think something is holding you back. Like you're obligated to be a certain way for your dad. And he feels like he should be a certain way for the church." He uses air quotes around *the church.* "And the church feels like they should be a certain way for God. It's just . . . isn't God all open arms and welcome home?"

"God, yes. People—well, sometimes yes, sometimes no. People are the hard part of being human."

"But that's my point. Why do all that for them when they judge you?"

"Do all what?" I demand.

"Change clothes. Best face forward. Smile on Sundays. Take their bullshit judgment. You know, pretend to be something you're not."

He has evidently been around long enough to assemble an accurate picture of how people perceive me. I zip my bag, all the Davey-inspired clothes inside, and climb into the front seat. "I don't know. I guess I'm scared."

"Of?"

"What everyone is scared of—that if I'm me, I'm not enough."

He's silent for a few miles, thinking. Maybe he wonders why. Maybe I do too. The harder he thinks, the slower we go. I put a stop to that. "Can you please solve the problems of the world and use the speedometer simultaneously?"

He more than makes up for the loss of speed. I barely have time to consider how tonight has changed something fundamental in the way I see Davey before we pass Molly the Corn Dolly and then we are in my driveway. What has changed us? Conversations? Meeting his friends? Getting out of town? Me kissing a girl? Those solutions seem too simple, too on the nose.

Guinevere and I are home at five minutes to twelve.

We're idling in the driveway—that lingering moment when the night is supposed to be over but it's not. I should go. Dad's waiting. Davey stares into my garage, because I am evidently the only one capable of lowering the door. All my art is on display for Otters Holt.

"You're enough," he says.

I say, "You too," and find that I'm pleased Davey is my friend now rather than just Mash's cousin.

Elizabeth McCaffrey, born 1999—d. ? IN LOVING MEMORY: She collected the best people.

Davey carts Guinevere to the corner of the garage for me; she fared well considering it was her first time in public. Before he climbs into the Camaro, he twists out of his sweater and tie and tosses them into the trunk. He's standing half-naked in my driveway, looking ridiculously handsome. Davey has a very nice chest. It's considerably nicer than Woods's, because Woods lifts dry-erase markers and peppermint tea, and Davey lifts . . . I don't know . . . Thomas.

Thomas. Thomas. Thomas.

I pick up his band shirt from the Daily Sit. "You're forgetting something," I say, and throw it into his palm like a quarterback.

"Well, I'm off," he says. Up-nod.

"You're off," I say. Up-nod.

That departure felt very two steps forward, three steps back.

Inside, I tiptoe toward the crack of light under Mom and Dad's door, checking my reflection in a hall mirror. Not good. Ear against the wood, I don't hear anything. I knock, praying for low lights and shadows.

"Enter," Dad says.

I am in full explanation mode before I move from hardwood to carpet, a room more his than hers. *I had a good time. We aren't in a ditch. I've already been here for five minutes.*

Mom lowers her sketchpad, pulls the covers closer to her chin, and checks with my dad before using a very calm but firm tone. "When we gave you permission to go with Davey, we thought he'd be returning you well before midnight."

Dad's working out my appearance. He is particularly

interested in my hair until he lights on my chin. Or is it my lips? Does he somehow know I kissed Gerry? He asks, "What's wrong with your neck?"

The Adam's apple. I cup my hand over the makeup. "Just a joke," I say, and then move on to Mom. "I was with *Davey*."

They don't seem nearly as impressed by Davey as they were earlier today. Their eyes flick from the digital clock on the nightstand to my neck. Dad removes his Bible-reading bifocals, gestures to me, and says to Mom, "I'm sure that'll make the morning paper."

"Oh, Scott. Stop it." Mom swats his arm as if this is the follow-up to an earlier conversation. She turns off their light and shoos me to bed with her eyes. When I'm halfway down the hall, her voice follows. "Don't forget the garage door."

That night, I dream I'm flying an Audi. Gerry's riding shotgun. Davey's wearing ten ties in the backseat and Audi Thomas has installed an espresso machine in the trunk. He's pouring glasses. Gerry rips out the front seat, tosses it out the window. It doesn't drop. It flies away like a bird. The rest of the seats go the same way. Suddenly, the Audi is large enough to hold a dance party of four. We jump. We kiss. The horn sings, "I cannot be contained." Gerry laughingly says, "We are more ambitious than a love triangle. We're a love square."

I wake up drenched in a fresh wave of worry over all the love squares in my life.

My best friend is in love with my other best friend. I'm going to have to deal with that at some point.

5

Davey's Part

THREE MONTHS EARLIER

He called me before I called him. Thom Cahill had a knack for three things: stealing my girlfriends, stealing my girlfriends in such a way that I ended up thinking they were better off with him than they were with me, and calling before I needed him.

Two hours before we'd left summer football workout together, and everything on my emotional monitor registered as level and fine. "How's it hanging, Winters?" he greeted me over the phone.

"At my feet," I told him.

"Meet at Bonjo?" he asked.

"Meet at Bonjo," I replied.

Fifteen minutes later, Thom and I were among the hipsters and writers who populated our favorite caffeinated haunt. Our barista had the day off, but even the second-string made us two Americanos before we asked for them. Impressed, I dropped an extra ten in the jar. A middle-aged lady with a baby abandoned our favorite table as if Thom had sent a text ahead asking her to vacate. The stage was set. Serious conversation to follow.

Thom twisted the square Waylan Academy ring he always wore on his pinkie because it was too small for his ring finger. The platinum gleamed against his skin. He'd had it polished again.

"You need something." He sounded sure of himself, which he always was. Being sure was a Thom thing— courtesy of a lifetime of being lavishly loved.

He sipped the coffee, and I had a vision of us doing this same thing when we were thirty. He'd chatter happily about his wife wanting him to work fewer hours at the firm, and I'd tell him my daughter spit up on my favorite tie. We'd be rich and annoying. Or we would at least pretend to be rich at thirty, which was annoying. But then the image glitches, and fuzzes like an old television, thanks to John Winters, my father.

Thom had called me two weeks before under similar circumstances. We'd talked about Mom catching Dad with Kaitlyn ("with a Y"), *his trainer*. We'd discussed the coming shitstorm. Two hours ago, that shitstorm made landfall in Casa Winters.

Thom asked, "What's the current situation?"

In his early forties (or perhaps before), my father developed a love of working out at expensive gyms. He likes women who know their way around a barbell; he likes toweling off in front of large mirrors. My mom has Betty Crocker hips, Sara Lee thighs, and Mother Teresa's devotion. They were never a very good match and hadn't been happy together in years, if ever. I used to obsess over them and my unfortunate role in their continuing relationship. I have since, with Thom's coaching, learned some distance. Also, my parents met when Mom was seventeen. My age.

"We're leaving him," I told Thom.

He accepted this pronouncement as I had, without question. "To where?" was the question. He asked it quietly, already suspecting this was the reason his Spidey sense had urged him to call.

During the family meeting, I'd requested this information too. I'd expected, oh, maybe a condo in Green Hills, there's a place showing in Lennox Village, I have a friend with a lovely bungalow in East. We'd move from swanky Brentwood, Tennessee, to greater Nashville, Tennessee. Good-bye, cheater. Hello, alimony.

"Otters Holt. Kentucky." I didn't hide my disdain, having holidayed there occasionally.

"That's where they have the very large yellow thing. What is it? A scarecrow?" he asked kindly.

"Molly the Corn Dolly," I responded with as much

enthusiasm as I could manage.

"Yes, Molly the Corn Dolly," Thom repeated, hiding a smirk behind his mug.

He was right to smirk. My grandfather had that thing constructed, but I'd never managed to tell anyone about it with a straight face, let alone Thom, who found the humor in most things. He did not find any humor in his best friend spending his senior year in a town that didn't even have a McDonald's. I tipped my mug on its rim, having already thought well beyond the absence of chain restaurants. Graduating elsewhere. Graduating away from Thom. Graduating from Otters Holt. How could I put that on a college application and be taken seriously?

Small towns (population 2,876, according to the sign next to Molly) were made of nosy people, and I wasn't village fare. Add to that I was a niche of a niche, and it had taken years to find friends who liked ties, intensity, and costumes.

Thom brooded over my brooding. We were the same age, but he'd always treated me like a little brother. I never once minded this. No one bloodied my nose with Thom around, and I always had someone next to me to ask the really important questions. The ring circumnavigated his finger. I twisted my own in unison, as if we might unlock a secret portal that did not involve me moving to Podunk.

"David, I'm going to break this to you gently: this situation sucks hairy gorilla balls, and you might die a young death of boredom or, at a minimum, never be allowed back into academia."

He said this because I wanted to hear it.

"That was a joke," he said.

"Not to me."

"David, it's not Outer Mongolia. We'll be what . . . two hours away?"

More like an hour and a half in the Audi. This was his way of saying he wouldn't leave me to the country mice. "It's a year. You can do anything for a year, yes?"

"It's a prison sentence. All because my dad got sweaty on Kaitlyn with a *Y*."

"Your dad got sweaty on Marnie with an *M*, and Ainsley with an *A*, and Rhonda like a rumba," he reminded me. "You can't blame your mom."

I didn't. Nor did I condone Dad's conduct. All this time, I'd known my mom might not get Botox injections or wear high heels to the gym, but her backbone was toned and muscular. I just hadn't expected her to move me to Outer Mongolia when she found out. Thom and I had planned to out Dad next year from the safety of a college dorm. Then she could hit him upside the head with a frying pan and everyone would have plausible deniability.

Thom switched tactics again. "Your cousin is there, right?"

"Yeah, Mash. He's all right, but Thom, end of the day, they're not like us."

"So your cousin is one of those aliens from *Terminator*? A mermaid? Half horse?"

"Yes," I said. "He's half horse and his group of friends are talking narwhals."

Thom clapped loudly enough that a man nearby lowered his newspaper and scowled. "There's one school for the *county*," I told Thom. Otters Holt felt exotic to me. Very third world. Nashville was awash with magnet schools, private schools, and specialized academies. Families didn't have to be *very* rich to send kids on this educational path, just very dedicated. My parents had been very dedicated; Thom's parents, by way of Thom's grandparents, were very rich. But neither of us had much experience with women. Waylan's lower and middle schools were all-boys as well.

Thom tapped his mug, counting aloud to eight, and said, "Eight hours of ladies *or* gentlemen, good sir. This will increase your odds of coitus by a factor of at least five. Ruminate on that advantage."

"You want me to find a country girl to have sex with?" I asked, as this seemed very unlikely.

"Yes, and I want her to call you darlin' and you to call her sweet pea, and the two of you to buy a lifetime supply of overalls from Carhartt. If you don't get Daisy Mae pregnant in three months, I'll be devastated." I nearly smiled, and he laughed for my benefit.

"When I visit my granddad, I live on my computer," I said as if it were a solution, a dismissal of dating anyone or finding friends. "You remember when we watched all those dog videos?"

"Dude, you can't watch dog videos for a year."

"What am I supposed to do?"

"I want you to figure out how 'happiness' works in Otters Holt. Happiness is a noun, David. Shall we go and look it up?"

We had a rare books section at the Waylan Academy library. There was a partial Oxford Dictionary collection from 1884. One of Thom's favorite "games" in junior high involved me stopping whatever I was doing and following him to the library, where he would look up a mundane word—*happiness, fear, worry*—and read the definition aloud in an English accent. Charming as hell, he'd cock his head to the side and repeat, "Happiness, noun, the state of being happy." I'd then counter-argue that he should look up *happy*, and we'd be caught in a loop of words and fake accents, which meant nothing except that we were dorks.

"Happiness is an emotion," I groaned.

"Of which you are capable. I've witnessed the phenomenon."

"Well, if you transform Otters Holt into LaserCon, that will be fine," I said. LaserCon was a large but local cosplay conference we had attended since we were old enough to insist our fire-retardant Spider-Man pajamas were costumes. Thom even hosted the occasional costume party dates here at Bonjo. Pop culture nerds need other pop culture nerds.

I suspected he also planned these parties at times when I was the most keyed up—near a big game, after a failed date, when my father was cruel.

He began, "I could throw a party there, but I don't think I can—"

Then I *hmm*ed. All my truly ingenious ideas sounded like engines.

"What's with the *hmm*-ing?"

"My dad's not going with us," I said.

"I rather think not."

"So I might be there, but I won't be subject to his rules anymore."

John Winters loves me. But he loves the idea of turning me into him more. On more than one occasion, I'd let him. Without his influence, I could breathe.

"You can be whoever you want there."

"Hell, I can be myself," I said.

Maybe I could put my intensity to work on something other than lacrosse or grades. I could experiment with who I was when the overlord departed the kingdom. I wasn't anxious to try this apart from Thom, but I was suddenly anxious for freedom I'd never had.

Thom smiled easily, and told me he would purchase a cookie of any size or variety if I could find the real David Winters within a ten-mile radius of Molly the Corn Dolly. He twisted his Waylan ring again. "New self. New name? You can even be Davey there if you want."

"Big T already calls me Davey."

"Okay then. Old place. Old name. Davey Winters. God, that sounds like you're picking hay already."

"I believe you bale hay," I said.

"See, you're already getting the hang of things."

6

A typical church day looks like this for me: doughnuts, Sunday school, church service, lunch, homework, youth group. A typical church day for Dad looks like this: work, work, extra meetings, work, more work. Today, there are two extra meetings: one with the deacons, one with the youth group parents.

I offer to attend the parents' meeting, to apologize. Thankfully, he declines. "At the end of the day, I'm the one responsible. It happened on my watch," he says.

The parsonage phone has rung off the hook all week. The other deacons are churning milk into cream. I overheard the words "fired" and "Brother Scott" and they were not in reference to flames. Two parishioners stopped me at the BI-LO this week—one sympathetic, one gossipy. I was buying broccoli for

Mom. "Bless your heart. I'll bet it's hard to be at the center of things." And in the frozen foods aisle. "That article in the paper true?"

Then, when I was bent over, running my thumb over a Hershey's bar to check for maximum almonds, two plump ladies had a conversation at my expense. "We'll just see how Brother Scott disciplines his daughter this time," they said. "That Miller girl's involved too," they hinted. "Those two are up to no good," they speculated.

As if Janie Lee and I were alone in that youth room with a blowtorch.

I expect more of the same today.

Sunday School is held in the basement fellowship hall instead of the youth room. The youth could stomach the destruction—big fans have been drying the water damage all week. Right after the opening prayer, Dad said, "Everyone better be here tonight. After I talk to your parents, we're discussing the incident. In detail."

Janie Lee turns a wicked shade of green at his sternness, which makes me want to Bubble Wrap her. My dad's the closest thing to a father figure she has. She's been partially grounded all week, logging hours at Bleach because of the newspaper article. Attention means skittish customers, and skittish customers make for an unhappy Mrs. Miller. The rest of the Hexagon looks equally uncomfortable.

But by Sunday night, Janie Lee isn't the only one who could use some Bubble Wrap. I make the mistake of sitting outside the meeting room and listening to the deacons whale on Dad, skittering around the corner only just before the first wave of them pours from the room, mouths still foaming with verbal rabies. I count to one hundred, slow my heartbeat, and take the back stairs to Youth Suite 201.

The fans are still blowing. Teens mill about, heading in and out of the suite, trying to sneak food before dinnertime. Woods Carrington hangs from the doorframe of 201, blocking anyone who wants to enter. He winks at me. I wink back. And there we are caught up in a moment of closeness even though we are fifteen feet apart.

"Billie, Woods, time to start," Dad yells.

Let Come-to-Jesus-Scott-McCaffrey time commence. Youth Suite 201 used to be swathed in mauve, cheap Ten Commandments posters, and four billion copies of a mini-magazine called *The Upper Room*. Dad caused quite a stir when he gifted the room to teenagers; he practically split the church when he allowed us to decorate it during a lock-in. It was Big T who wrote that check and patted the cheeks of enough deacons so that they finally shut their grumbling faces.

It's currently a livable dwelling for people my age, i.e., Xbox, Ping-Pong table, snacks.

Dad's currently livid. He's retrieving a stack of Bibles from the window ledge. "You all better buckle up." He has erased THINGS TO DO WITH A CHURCH MICROWAVE and written a scripture reference.

Einstein bears two gray battle smudges on its otherwise

white surface. The right side of the frame is melted. There in the bottom corner, the stick drawing of me holding the Corn Dolly has survived explosions, sprinklers, and Scott McCaffrey. You can just make out *Harvest Festival Forever*.

Dad sets Bibles at our feet and taps the board. *Tap. Tap. Tap.* Woods squirms—the desire to wrestle the marker from Dad nearly consumes him.

"He really has no idea what he has," Woods whispers to me.

"Clearly," I say, because this power struggle delights me.

Dad underlines the scripture, a cue for everyone to thumb to the address. My Bible is propped unopened on my lap. I have no room to hear the book of Hebrews because Woods says, "Did I tell you Wilma Frist confirmed this year's the last Harvest Festival? No more speculation."

I shake my head, disturbed by this information on a gut level. Woods is moving a Blow Pop from one side of his mouth to the other. He looks as if he's considering Hebrews instead of this terrible news.

No Harvest Festival means no Corn Dolly. For a town that has a forty-foot-tall roadside attraction—one that comes up on the home page when you google Kentucky—the idea of discontinuing the Harvest Festival, and the Corn Dolly celebration, sounds preposterous.

The Corn Dolly may sound like a joke, but at its heart, it's nothing to snicker at. My Grandy was the Corn Dolly winner of 1979, and how she won is a story that my father has recounted more times than he's told the resurrection of Jesus. (It kills him that my mom has never been nominated.) The story begins, "1979 was the year of the flood," and ends with "And that's how Grandy changed everything."

Otters Holt is on a verdant strip of land between Lake Barkley and Kentucky Lake. Both lakes are man-made, fed by the Tennessee River, and gorgeous. When I was a kid I combined robin's-egg and cornflower blue, attempting to color the exact shade of Kentucky Lake. "You're missing the magic," Mom had said over my shoulder. And I was. Nothing in robin's-egg or cornflower spoke to the true beauty of water and sky and brown, crag-filled shoreline.

All that enchantment is fine and good if it doesn't rain too much. Spring of 1979 it rained more than too much.

Grandy said school let out so kids could sandbag houses. She's also fond of exaggerating: "The only thing we had more of than sandbags were *Road Closed* signs. Borrowed them from six other counties to have enough." The campgrounds closed; the bison had to be moved to another park. And there was Grandy, bagging, baking, and bed-and-breakfasting ten extra people whose homes were afloat on the Tennessee. (No exaggeration there.) That wasn't what clenched the Corn Dolly of 1979, though. Everyone helped everyone. As we do. Grandy went above and beyond.

The kid of one of her friends got caught in some quicksand and died. After the water receded, Grandy raised five thousand dollars so her friend could put a down payment on a home miles away from the waterfront. "These lakes are beautiful, but water will turn on you, Billie, and when it does, beauty ain't what you see anymore." I must have heard Grandy tell that story three hundred times. I never get tired of it.

That kind of stellar living and giving awards you a Corn Dolly. Every year, there is a story just like this one.

I think about Grandy. I think about *Harvest Festival Forever*. I think about Big T. I think about Molly the Corn Dolly. I think: *No. No, I will not let this be the end of a good thing.*

"Can you believe that phrase *Harvest Festival Forever* survived?" I'm whispering at Woods, but Dad sets his laser eyes upon us, and taps his Bible to remind us of the task.

I flick my finger at the speech bubble.

Woods cocks his head, stares at Einstein, sees the meaning I intend. "Are you thinking what I'm thinking?" he asks.

I pretend to check a page in Woods's Bible, but really, I'm baiting him. "You could keep it going."

"Without Tyson?" he asks.

Good question. The Harvest Festival, the Corn Dolly, and the Sadie Hawkins dance—the hat trick of Otters Holt—have always been funded and largely spearheaded by Tyson Vilmer.

"Are you or are you not Woods Carrington, future mayor of Otters Holt?"

He's unconvinced but intrigued. I'm determined.

"You two have something more interesting to contribute than the Apostle Paul?" Dad asks.

Preacher's-kid fast, I answer, "I was thinking about Queen Esther." Dad doesn't believe me, so while I'm staring at

Woods, I quote rather convincingly, "'I've come into the kingdom for such a time as this.'"

Woods hears the message loud and clear. I get a pat on the knee. With Woods on task, the festival is as good as saved.

Still, there's a reckoning to come. Everyone in the room is parked in Hebrews and waiting for the smackdown except me, so Dad asks, "Billie, you want to read for us?"

"I will, Brother Scott," Janie Lee volunteers.

Bless her. He allows her rescue mission, but not without passing judgment that would make a Pharisee proud. Janie Lee begins to read. The paraphrase: Discipline is painful in the moment, but it helps people—the "us" is implied—grow into decent human beings. The translation: We are not yet decent human beings, but we will be when Dad finishes with our punishment.

"Do you know what that means?" asks Brother Scott.

Fifty answers, "It means you're pissed."

"Decent guess." Dad goes on to explain that in his "cooldown period" he concluded there's not enough yelling in the universe to repair the church. I was unaware of this cool-down period.

"Here's what you're going to do," he instructs. "There are elderly people in our church who need help with things. You are going to do *all* those things. Construction for destruction. Help in exchange for harm. There will be no argument. No attitude." He eye-checks the two he expects to be rebels, Fifty and me. "And when things square with the insurance people, we'll reassess whether I need to take another section of your hindquarters. *Capisce?*"

I'm rendered speechless. Manual labor is a step down from Filet o' Billie. This actually makes sense.

"What about those of us who *weren't* in the youth room when the fire started?" asks a freshman. The dude's best friend parrots, "Yeah. What about us?"

Fifty digs into the couch cushions, finds a yellow crayon, and hurls it at them. "Then you missed out."

"Seriously?" the boy asks. "Why should the rest of us do nice things for old people?"

"Rewind that question and ask it again in slow motion," I say.

Dad can't decide whether he's proud of me or aggravated. In the end, he skips my comment and says, "You're a group. That's how we're doing this."

God's servant has spoken, and I agree with the commandment. I never meant to hurt the church in the first place. Bring on the gerontological penance. Brother Scott tells us we'll receive our assignments in the mail after he has consulted the elderly.

With that handled, we have a typical Sunday night. Bible is studied. Games are played. Ice cream is consumed straight from the carton.

Dad can be tough, but he really does love us enough to buy mint chocolate chip.

7

We're still lingering in the youth room doing what we normally do after meeting: talk shit, play Ping-Pong, avoid weekend homework. Dad's in his office doing whatever Dad does in his office. Perhaps he's writing next week's sermon. Or assigning us old people. Or praying he gets those mumbling deacons to extend some grace after we aerate their lawns and re-roof their sheds.

Woods is over the moon about this punishment. He's already twirled me in circles and given me three bullet reasons we win the world. 1) Our ass isn't grass. 2) Old people are awesome. 3) Old people are awesome.

"You know you repeated yourself, right?" I ask, as soon as my equilibrium stops spinning.

"That was for effect," he argues.

Fifty pets his beard into submission and gets an idea. "I dare you to write those three bullets, verbatim, *ass* and all, on Einstein," and Woods and I both cut eyes at Dad's office and say, "And then we stop winning the world."

"When you two get married, I'm not coming," Fifty says.

Thinking only of Fifty bucking plans, not the actual plan he listed, I say, "Yes, you will." Woods chooses to echo my exact words again, and we realize what we've said at the same moment.

Two faces go red. Awkward descends. We stop touching and drift to opposite sides of the room. I check to see if Janie Lee heard us. No, she's playing Jenga with Mash and Davey. This can't be the first time someone has joked about us being together. But it's the first time since Janie Lee has declared her intentions.

I drift over to Einstein and try to concentrate on my plan to save the Harvest Festival. Unsuccessfully. I am not a bad friend. I can contain my feelings for Woods. I will not lose the Hexagon with a selfish misstep.

Around me are voices: *Billie, who's going to get paired up? Billie, what happens if he asks me to work during band practice? Billie, Billie, Billie* . . . No one will let me stay inside my head. Janie Lee nudges my legs to the floor and takes up residency in my lap, bringing her blanket along. She was a cat in her former life.

"Yes?" I say, my attention now fully gathered.

I've never really understood the appeal of playing with someone's hair, but Janie Lee can hardly keep from it. She twirls a lock of my hair around her finger. "You protected me from Brother Scott after all."

Not true. He decided to go light on his own. But I say, "I tranq-ed him last night. Dart gun to the head. *Pow*. Then two hours of waterboarding and . . . voilà."

"You two should kiss and get it over with," Fifty says. "Or maybe you don't want to steal the show from Davey and *Thomas*."

Clearly, everything is sexual to Fifty. If I got turned on every time Janie Lee crawled in my lap or Woods turned me in a circle, I'd be in trouble.

"Maybe we will, asshole," Janie Lee says playfully. "Maybe we will." She nods at me, urging me to affirm this declaration. Unsure of what to do, I look at Woods, who looks at Mash, who looks back to Davey.

Chain reaction. Davey reacts so I don't have to. He collects his cell from the basket and shakes his jeans to proper hip placement. Nothing he owns fits him. I presume he means to leave, but I want him here to put my Corn Dolly plan in motion. We're finally down to just the Hexagon in the room. Wordlessly, I beg Woods to compel everyone to stay. He pauses Ping-Pong, quick-walks to the door, closes it, gives everyone a cocky lip curl like he has a secret he won't tell us unless we're on the couch. Davey stays put near the door.

Woods makes a show of leaning toward Dad's office and checking the hallway. He crosses the room and peers out the windows to the parking lot. Total déjà vu.

"Coast is clear," he announces. "Billie, the floor is yours."

I stand, carefully dumping Janie Lee to the carpet. "May I?" I ask, before picking up the dry-erase marker.

Woods grants permission. "You may indeed."

We bow at each other and take positions on either side of Einstein. I circle the entirety of the bottom picture. "Do you know why this is still here?" I ask the group.

When no one says anything, Woods says, "Come on, Hexagon. Out with your answers. One of your own has spoken."

"Because your dad didn't erase it?"

"Because Fifty drew it in Sharpie?"

"Because the fire seared it into the board?"

"Because Mash puked on it?"

I need Woods to be the one to say this to everyone. "Because it's still important," he announces on cue.

One finger to my nose, one finger aiming at Woods, I say, "Exactly. You guys, this little drawing is a miracle. We have to treat this"—I tap *Harvest Festival Forever*—"like an epiphany."

Fifty's mouth is cockeyed with objections. He works his toothpick from side to side, states a fact. "Billie, that drawing was me dicking around. Teenagers like . . ." He means to say me, but he course-corrects, "Yo, teenagers can't win the Corn Dolly. Lost cause."

"Hold up," I say. "This isn't about me winning the Corn Dolly. Woods, tell them what you heard."

So he does. He explains how he was having breakfast with

his geezer crew at the Fork and Spoon, and Wilma Frist said the Harvest Festival is caput and defunct without Tyson Vilmer's financial support. Old men passed the old women their handkerchiefs. Everyone had moist eyes, a moment of nostalgia. Then people salted their eggs and sipped their black coffee. Everyone in that crew already has a Corn Dolly or is married to a recipient. They've checked that box. End accepted.

Not me.

In some ways my whole life has been a flight of steps to the outer world. That's when I'll stride through the door of graduation into the jungle. Maybe to Nashville. Maybe to New York. Maybe to Charlotte, North Carolina, because Davidson College is there and they have a great art program.

Out there, the questions will be different, the people larger-minded. For four years, I'll live a life outside the glass bowl of church and Scott McCaffrey. Out there, I might be straight or gay or bi, conservative or liberal, Christian or Buddhist, or . . . anything. Out there, I choose. No one cares whether I wear jeans or dresses. It'll feel like jumping in a coffee shop to a song called "I Cannot Be Contained."

Because those fictitious future people will raise a glass at my oddities. They'll say, "Tell me about growing up," and I'll say, "The year I was seventeen, I had five best friends—a pixie, a president, a pretender, a puker, and a douchebag—and I was in love with all of them for different reasons. They'll ask where, and I'll tell them Otters Holt. They'll know it. *That place with the huge yellow doll statue? Yes, and huge Harvest Festival,* I'll say, and then I'll stick out my chest and say with vigor, *And I'm going back there.*

I want the power to invent whatever me I desire, but I need to know I can come home and home will look like home.

Woods is wrapping up his case with, "It really all boils down to money. Big T wasn't just the heart, he was the wallet, and they can't see anyone else stepping up to take those reins. They're older, so the idea of fund-raising year after year isn't appealing."

Mash adds, "I heard Mom and Dad saying at lunch that his estate isn't what it used to be. They went through everything with Henry down at the bank and there's barely enough to pay off the farm."

Davey confirms.

"That's where we come in," Woods and I say together.

"Jinx," we say.

"Jinx, jinx," we say.

Janie Lee is the only one looking traitorously iffy. From the floor, she gives me a *this-won't-work-it's-dead-already* glare, to which I say, "Don't give me that cheeky look, Miller. They might not have the energy to fund-raise, but we do."

In truth, she won't stick around Otters Holt long enough to win a Corn Dolly. Not a girl in town can scrub the notion of winning from her head. Even if it isn't realistic.

The rest of them nod at us.

"How?" Mash asks.

Ceremoniously, I pass the marker to Woods and say, "Lead us, Jedi Master."

Woods writes WAYS TO SAVE THE HARVEST FESTIVAL atop the board.

Einstein crackles with new life.

Everyone talks at once.

"That sounds like work."

"We need to raise a shit ton of money."

"Money will fix everything."

"Should we wait until after the ballots come out?"

Woods addresses Fifty's concern first. "Sorry, lazy, you're doing this with us, even if we *are* overreacting." Then to Janie Lee and Mash he asks, "Fund-raising ideas?"

They present the usual suspects: bake sale, car wash, rent-a-kid—all things we've done at church. Woods paces the length of the room, staring at Einstein during each pass, as if the answers are written in invisible ink.

Davey reminds us Brother Scott is already renting out youth free of charge and none of us bakes.

"You could sell that Camaro," Fifty suggests.

"You could sell that beard," Davey says back.

I'm relieved to see Davey challenge him. Woods, not so much. "Guys, not the time. Bigger fish frying."

The best thing to do for Davey and Fifty is stay on topic, so I say, "A donation isn't best. We don't need one person involved. There's not another Big T in town except for Tawny, and that old goat won't give us a dime. We need the whole community."

Mash says, "Game over," and makes a deflated video game sound. "No one will listen to us anyway. We just set the church on fire."

Still, Woods writes *Multiple Donations* as a bullet point. Tapping the board, he says, "So, this isn't our usual challenge, Hexagon. Nut up. We need to make this happen. Think of the redemption."

"Do you think who wins has any bearing on it continuing?" Mash asks.

Theories erupt.

"It might be better if Tawny wins. She could fund the festival."

"If might be better if Tawny loses. She'll want to win next year and might donate enough to keep it going."

"What about Billie's mom, Clare? She has the backing of the church."

"Brother Scott could get people to donate."

"Hello, dufus, Brother Scott is in a fix because of the fire."

Davey reads my mind, speaks. "Let's not worry about pre-determining the winner. We don't even know who's on the ballot yet. I say we give the town something that reminds them who they are."

"They?" Fifty asks.

Caught in this act of treason, Davey corrects himself. "We."

Woods asks for more details. Davey gives them. He is logical, concise. "When I was a kid, the Harvest Festival was at the elementary school. That's where it started, right?" Everyone nods. Before it moved to Vilmer's Barn, the school hosted the festival. "So we clean up the elementary school grounds. We revitalize a piece of history. The older generations will love the antiquity. The new generation will have ownership."

The elementary school? I love that old ruin. And it has been the subject of much debate in the newspaper. The property is an eyesore, but a landmark, too. He's right. Cleaning it up is a solid idea. Time-wise, I'm unsure if we can pull it off. Five weeks isn't long.

Woods determines five weeks is plenty long enough to work a miracle. He offers the marker and Davey accepts. Before Davey proceeds, he strokes the front of his T-shirt as if he misses his tie.

"How does that raise money?" Janie Lee asks.

"Like I said, we clean up the elementary school. All of us. We plant flowers, landscape, revitalize. Then, we host some sort of game on the field a week before the festival. A community event. Something that anyone can play. Like kickball. Or Wiffle ball. And we sell tickets, cheap. But if we sell enough of them—"

"You want kickball to be the savior of the Harvest Festival?" Fifty asks. "They teach you that at Waylan Academy?"

Davey backs down at the mention of his old school. "I'm only trying to help."

"I want to believe you, except . . ." Fifty uses a pregnant pause and gestures to the room. "Everyone knows you're serving time here, I'm just asshole enough to call you on it. You're always on your cell with Thomas instead of hanging with us. And that's fine and all, but don't act like our savior now." He's pulling at his beard, just below his chin. Large sweat rings line his armpits. "Woods, dude, come up with something better."

"Fifty, chill." Woods's words are sharp. To Davey, he says, "Tell us more about kickball."

Mash says, "Let's call it KickFall," and is genuinely surprised when Davey writes it down.

Within minutes there are five bullets below MULTIPLE DONATIONS.

- Clean up school: bush hog, mow, drag field, repair playground, landscape
- Sell KickFall tickets for $2/raise $2000/1000 people to attend
- Door-to-door recruiting/announce at football game
- KickFall game: before Corn Dolly vote/food & drinks—ask church ladies
- Flowers?

When Fifty thinks no one is looking, his lips part in a smile. I am unsure whether he was a dick to rile Davey up, or because Fifty is Fifty. Based on that knowing expression, I'm leaning toward riling. "You really believe you can save the festival?" he asks Woods.

"Absolutely."

"Want to bet on it?" Fifty asks.

Everyone *oooohs*, knowing exactly what he's going to say. Janie Lee rockets a pillow at his head, and says what he wants to hear. "Robert Fifty Tilghman, if we raise two thousand dollars on KickFall, I solemnly swear to you the whole Hexagon will walk Vilmer's Beam." Janie Lee is a master at knowing who responds to what. Woods is nodding at the approach. At her strategy. Maybe he's nodding at more than that.

Fifty pops up to full height. "No shit, J-Mill?"

He has advocated relentlessly for this particular group activity every time we're in sight of the barn. And often when we are not. All because Fifty was out of town the weekend we were stupid enough to walk it in middle school, and he has been hell-bent ever since.

"No shit," Janie Lee says.

Woods adds to Einstein, ADDITIONAL STAKES = $2000 OR HEXAGON WALK VILMER'S BEAM.

Game on.

8

"You really shouldn't do that in sunglasses," Janie Lee says.

That is operating my band saw, which is technically Dad's band saw, but the ability to turn it on is nine-tenths of ownership.

"I belong to a small tribe of people who don't like to do anything without sunglasses," I tell her. My clear safety glasses are elsewhere, and I'm too focused to stop. We have fifteen minutes before Davey picks us up for Service Projects: Super Saturday, and I intend to make the most of them. God knows I've had no time to work this week.

"You're going to belong to a small tribe of people without thumbs," she warns.

I *pshhh* this notion. The garage door is up. Light lazes about like it has nothing better to do than disrupt shadows, and I've already stripped down to a tank top because where there's light, there's heat. And where there's Billie, there's sawdust.

"You should teach me sometime."

Before she arrived, I discovered the Daily Sit was in need of an interior frame to be structurally sound. Since she's longing for an invitation, I say, "Come here to me," and Janie Lee snaps her violin safely away and places it near the door where she won't forget it later. Then, we are standing at the saw, me dressing her in sunglasses—they're a little too small—looking uncertain, adorable. Maybe even excited.

I place a scrap of wood in her hands while she complains. "Billie, be careful with me. I'm shit for this work."

I circle her like a dad teaching a kid to hit a baseball, and together we run wood through the saw. A fine spray of pine coats the front of her sweatshirt and my glasses. She runs the line straight. I flip the switch to off, clear the board, and wipe her glasses clean. She is dusty and lingering, as if she's forgotten everything except me and the two-by-four. I force her to smell the tips of her fingers. "Smell that?" I ask.

Freshly sawed art. Perfect lines. Ahhhhh. After inspecting the raw edges of the wood and assessing how it will fit into the larger picture of the Daily Sit, she says, "For all the times your ideas get us in trouble, I'm still in love with your brain."

I like it when she says stuff like this. Mainly because she's one of those annoying people who doesn't start things she can't finish and yet we get on so charmingly. "Shoot, Miller, don't get gooey on me. I'm only training you up for your geronto-logical punishment."

I knock rogue sawdust from the front of my shirt and from hers. I imagine what would happen if this were Woods and her in a half-lit garage. If that flick of the wrist across her chest might become more. Maybe a hand in the small of her back. Palm touching soft skin. Yes, I think it would.

Janie Lee returns my glasses, resettles herself on the freezer, and continues the conversation. "I highly doubt Tawny Jacobs will need me to saw anything."

"The dreams of small children?" I suggest.

"She's not that bad. We had a good week."

This is a very Janie Lee way to feel. Tawny's the only woman in Otters Holt to be nominated ten times for the Corn Dolly and never win. Way back when, she baked pies and gave away *whole* Snickers bars for Halloween. But now, she's Otters Holt's very own Miss Havisham.

The entire youth group got called in to trim trees and pick pecans at Tawny's after school on Thursday. Her husband has been dead for sixty years, and she manages forty-one acres alone. If she weren't such a mean old biddy, I'd slap a sash around her chest that said Feminist of the Year. Every acre, save the one with her "homestead," is buried under a canopy of fruit- and nut-producing trees.

I'll say one thing for her. She is the owner of the best white perimeter fences in the whole damn county. Miles and miles of fences made for racing. If you've never raced fences with a best friend—on anything with wheels—you really haven't lived. Mash, Woods, Fifty, and I once hijacked two zero-turn mowers from Big T and raced them down the lane like it was the Indy 500, all while Tawny shook her broom on the front porch. The four of us have done quite a bit of living. Janie Lee, for the most part, has done quite a bit of watching. She doesn't go fast. Or honk her horn. Or throw gravel. Or hijack mowers. Not anymore.

She cheers for us and has 911 at the ready.

"*You* might have had a good week. She told *me* that dressing like a man attracts wanton attention," I say.

"What did you say to that?"

"Well, I wanted to tell her that if Jesus wore a skirt, I could wear pants."

"Billie—"

"I said wanted to. Don't worry, I thanked her kindly for the insight."

"How were things with Grandy?" she asks.

I low whistle. She didn't go easy on me. Tuesday after school, she sent me up the attic stairs to bring things down. "Just a little sorting," she promised. Forty-three boxes were given to Goodwill, although a few bearing "art supplies" landed in my garage. I did find a tin of Christmas cookies from 1999. Mash ate one on a dare. "I'm happy to say he didn't throw up," I tell Janie Lee.

We discuss the other assignments, how they're off to a rip-roaring success. How we feel as though we might be turning the tide regarding the opinion of Community Church Youth Group. It's a perfectly good conversation, until she mentions asking Woods to the Sadie Hawkins dance. I keep my commentary to a solitary statement. "You better be sure, because if you ask him, it changes everything."

"And that's why I haven't said anything yet," she admits. "There should be a manual for all this relationship shit."

"Truth," I say, lowering my glasses. I cut three more two-by-fours before Janie Lee interrupts me.

"Are you ever going to finish that thing?" She indicates Guinevere.

I pretend to be appalled. "The Daily Sit has my full attention."

I'm sort of famous for two things: unfinished projects and gifting ridiculous unfinished items. I once gave Woods a television made entirely of book covers. He has it hanging on the wall in his room. We watch it sometimes as if it's real. I like it better than cable.

"Maybe you should gift the couch to Davey," she says.

"Maybe I will."

There's still dust on her chest, over her heart. She swipes at it and says, "You know, you two would make a cute couple," without lifting her eyes.

I turn on the saw.

Five minutes later Davey turns up in my garage looking useful in his beat-up jeans and Waylan Academy Lacrosse T-shirt. There's faint purple eyeliner making his eyes pop and sparkle. The temperature is in a truly Kentucky mood, which means I grab a sweatshirt, just in case. It's morning, but he lies on the concrete floor, spread-eagle, and says, "We're never going to be done serving the old people." I nod, but he gives me an exasperated snarl. "What do you know? You're the Energizer Bunny. Do you ever get tired? No. You've probably been up working on that dang couch since midnight."

"It's true," Janie Lee agrees. "You are a bunny."

"See?"

His voice sounds Middle Tennessee today. More southern and long, instead of raw and slow. He's interesting. I wonder at the difference between interest and attraction. And if that's what's really going on with Janie Lee and Woods. Between me and Woods.

"I probably *should* get up at midnight if I ever want to finish this stupid couch," I say.

Even though I have to leave the Daily Sit to go do another service project, I'm excited to get out of the garage. Throwing tree limbs and mulch sounds therapeutic after thinking about Woods and Janie Lee dancing at the Harvest Festival. The last Harvest Festival probably, because there has been zero time to execute the plan written on Einstein.

Today's fire retribution is Wilma Frist, a pear-shaped woman who drives a light-pink Town Car that plays Christmas music year around. She's just the kind of woman I don't want to be when I grow up, but she's charming all the same. When we arrive, she's bubbling with the delight of someone who overprepares. Fifteen pair of gloves, shovels, hacksaws, and maps are spread out on her picnic table. (There are only six of us working.) Near the woods, there's a Dodge Ram full of mulch. ("My son Tony brought it over this morning.") She's filled a pitcher with yellow Gatorade. She explains what she wants done and ends her speech with "Make sure you hydrate," before retreating inside to observe us from the kitchen window.

No one is shocked when Woods offers additional instructions. Davey and I are to walk the trail and remove or saw the larger obstacles. Mash and Fifty will wheelbarrow and dump mulch at various places along the trail. Woods and Janie Lee will rake the smaller debris to the sides. Everyone spreads mulch at the end. This trail is a half mile in length. If we even get to mulch this morning, I'm going to be impressed.

"I have thirteen grandchildren, and I want this trail safe." Fifty uses his worst old-woman voice, and then his own. "If she has thirteen grandchildren, why aren't they doing this?"

"Because her thirteen grandchildren didn't set a church on fire," I remind him.

Woods and Janie Lee leave us, and Janie Lee gives me a discreet two-thumbs-up, as if I've planned these pairings. Their two forms, as seen from the back, are in the same flowing line I notice when they're playing music. Jealousy might be a shallow well, but I bend my face to it all the same and take a drink.

"You're stuck with me, McCaffrey," Davey says.

"More like Mash is stuck with Fifty." I tug Davey to the

other trailhead. This is a forest of poplars, oaks, and pines. Trunks are long; branches are high, each competing for sunlight at around one hundred feet. At eye level, everything is gray and brown, with the occasional splash of bright-green moss or deep-green pine. Every half mile or so, a forest like this lurks along the highway, planted by God and used by hunters. But Davey walks into an ambitious ray of sunshine and twirls circles like a princess in Disney World.

"You don't have parks in Nashville?" I ask.

"Nashville is relatively green. Waylan had a forest like this on campus. It"—he closes his eyes and breathes—"smells so good out here. I like this air."

I wrap my arm around a nearby tree, inhaling the sweetness of its bark, feeling thankful it does its CO_2 thing without me even noticing or asking. Below my feet are fallen leaves. Earth. I wonder: Does the soil on his old campus look this brown or is it tinted slightly red? I wonder: Is he someone who notices details? I wonder: Do we have other things in common?

"Are you going to keep hugging that tree?" he asks. "Or are we going to work?"

We've cleared four fallen trees and sawn through a fifth when Davey removes his long-sleeved T-shirt and hangs it on a branch. The Waylan jersey he's wearing beneath the sweatshirt looks old and lovely.

Across the woods, I make out the pink of Janie Lee's cap, hear her voice and Woods's making music. No doubt she's kicking leaves in those damn UGGs and having a perfect time.

I am staring at them, thinking complicated thoughts, when Davey says, "What was your question just then? The one you didn't ask."

I'd wanted to know if he played basketball at Waylan. Instead, I said, "Are you happy here?"

He affectionately pats a tree. "Wilma has nice woods. And this trail, when it's finished, will be—"

"You know that's not what I meant."

He sinks the saw teeth into a standing and healthy tree, works the flimsy blade back and forth until it's stuck.

"You can say."

"No," he argues.

"Why?"

He turns away from the tree, leaving the saw buried in oak. "Because this is your dreamland."

"And this is your what . . . punishment?" I ask.

When he doesn't answer, I poke. The words come out of me unplanned. "Is being mysterious and unknowable some sort of weird triumph for you?"

"I am not mysterious and unknowable."

I call foul. "You forget. I've seen you with your people. I know what you're like when you're not holding back. Come on. It's me. If you hate Otters Holt, you can say it."

The saw resists when he tries to jerk it from the tree. "I don't hate Otters Holt."

"But you miss Thom?"

"Of course. The same way you miss Janie Lee and Woods

when they're not tied to your side. Except they're right over there, and Thom is a decent drive away."

I walk over, bump him out of the way. "See. Now we're getting somewhere." He sidesteps my bravado, but the saw doesn't obey me any more than it obeyed him.

He taps me on the shoulder, formally, as if he'd like a dance. He says, "I'd like to tell you something."

"Well, I'd like the same," I say, looking from him to the saw.

"B, if something were going to happen between you, with either of them, I think it would have happened already. They live on one planet. You live on another. You should find someone who is your equal."

Either of them? He's not jabbing at me like Fifty. Not making a sexual comment just to make one. He's flinging open two doors instead of one. It's not something I can respond to yet. It's too fresh. I thought when he said he wanted to tell me something, it would be about him. "Why do you care if anything happens?" I say with more bite than I intend.

"I don't," he snaps back in a way that screams *I do.*

He called me B, the letter racing from his lips. I like that he sees the differences between them and me. But I have never thought myself unequal.

Half a football field away, Woods and Janie Lee round a bend in the trail, come into full view. His unruly hair falls so he has to brush it out of his eyes; hers, a straightened black drape, frames a heart-shaped face. Her arm's casually looped around his elbow; he's bent slightly, listening intently. They are a homecoming poster. I have to find something else to see.

Woods yells a greeting, which we ignore. Perhaps because they've interrupted something. Perhaps because we're hell-bound to remove the saw. They're still trumpeting out a pop song that will lodge in my head all day. They're louder. They're happier. They're coming closer with each step. Frustrated, I grab the wooden saw handle and plant both feet on the tree and pull.

"That's a bad id—"

I fly backward through the air. I'm flat on my back in the middle of the trail, saw in hand. Sudden laughter tumbles from my belly. Davey throws himself down next to me, hands balled around his mouth like a child from cackling so hard. It takes us a moment to grow still and quiet. His head lolls toward me. "I'm sorry," he says.

I roll sideways and lay my temple against the soft pillow of earth to see the apology in his eyes. They are blue—piercing, sorrowful—blue. "I am too."

He doesn't blink. "You know I meant you're better than them?"

I sidestep this compliment. "And you know you can trust me with unpopular opinions."

"She likes him and he likes her and you like them," he says, as if it's a mystery.

I flatten myself against the ground, wishing this were quicksand and I could disappear. His pinkie taps the ground. I feel the reverb. Cream and butter beams of light illuminate the tree we abused with the saw. I slip my hand into his and stare through the tinted lenses of my sunglasses. "She doesn't like him," I say. "She thinks she loves him. Maybe."

"And you're confused."

"Because . . ." Does he know?

"You can't tell which of them you love most anymore."

I hide my face inside my shirt. "Let's not use the love word, okay?"

"If that's what you want."

He's compliant because I asked, not because I've changed his mind. He sounds sad. And I suppose he is. A preacher's daughter should be comfortable with the L word.

He says, "I think there's a place where love equals history and a place where love equals the future and a place where love is just love and it doesn't go away no matter whether you get it back or not. Figuring out the difference—"

"Is impossible," I finish.

The singing is now nearly over the tops of our heads. Carefully, without discussion, we unclasp our fingers. There's no way to know from Woods's expression if he sees or not, because he's too busy busting our balls about lying down on the job. "We're slaving away out here and you two are making forest angels."

I say, "Being reprimanded by two people singing show tunes who haven't broken a sweat doesn't make me hop to my feet."

Davey and I separate enough to claim our own pieces of ground. We swing our legs and arms about wildly until we've moved the brush as if it were snow. While I'm still moving, I argue, "We've already done some serious work."

Woods looks at Davey, glares at me. Looks at Davey, scowls at me. "Oh, I can tell."

The tone warrants raising my sunglasses and a flash of my lizard eyes. Davey tenses. The staredown ends with Janie Lee's totally obtuse statement. "Aw, Billie, you look really happy."

Part of me takes flight and lands spritelike on a limb far above the forest, keen to observe the truth.

There is Woods. There is Janie Lee. There is Davey. There is me.

I do not know what type of love we are—history, future, or infinity—but we are love all the same. Welded strangely together like something in my garage. Like Guinevere or the unicorns. And we are just as unfinished.

9

With the semi-success of Operation Service Project, Dad offers me a short reprieve. Janie Lee is invited to a dinner of Cheetos, pizza, and Mom's very un-southern tea. When Mom and Dad start debating church politics at the table, Janie Lee and I escape to my room.

She takes the desk chair and opens her violin case. I settle on the bed with a box of Legos. For an hour, she plays, I build, and we are happier than two baby goats chewing on the same chunk of grass. We've always done silence as a deep conversation. In that span of time, I don't think of the future, or the past—I let myself breathe present air.

We are here, and I am comfortable.

Then, we are temple to temple watching *Saturday Night*

Live. Neither of us is a fan, so we flip the channel until we find Betty White.

And we are here, and I am comfortable.

At eleven, Mom knocks, and tells us not to stay up too late. "Church tomorrow, girlies," she reminds us. "Want me to flip the light?"

We do. The alarm clock's blue glow illuminates Janie Lee's shadowy image. She's wearing large-frame glasses, and pajamas I detest with holy passion. I smell honeysuckle—her face cream—that reminds me I am not particularly clean after a day of hard labor. I carry myself off to shower and return to find her still awake.

I grab a blanket I call the Sheep and toss it over her. Skip this step and experience says I'll wake up stripped of covers and shaking. I bury myself next to her, and she says, "You remember sophomore year?"

Sophomore year refers to one day in particular. My twin bed seems like a king. "Hey," I say warmly, and then her head, her tears, are on my chest. "No one thinks about that anymore."

The Tuesday after the Martin Luther King, Jr. holiday, thirty-five Otters Holt students found Marie Miller, Janie Lee's mom, on a desk in first-period chemistry. Naked. With Mr. Klinger. Also naked. The formaldehyde pig, Tog, was also a casualty. As were two Bunsen burners.

"Why are you even thinking about that?" I ask.

Janie Lee finds words. "Because she's why I don't date.

Why I'm afraid of asking Woods to the dance. Afraid of everything when it comes to relationships." She has never said these words before. Nor the ones that come after. "What if I'm like her? What if I miss out on someone like him because I can't—"

"Janie Lee, you might live in the same house, but you don't come from the same place."

"But so many people think of her, of that, when they see me. Eleven months. Eleven months." She repeats her mantra several more times.

"A) You aren't in their brains, so who knows? And B) You can leave Otters Holt in eleven months, buddy, but you'll pack that fear in your suitcase unless you realize you aren't like her."

"That's easy for you to say. Your mom is Corn Dolly material."

"Maybe, but that doesn't make me wrong."

She's worried she'll turn out like her mom; I'm worried I won't. Somehow my introverted mother has mastered the art of marching to her own drum in a rhythm people appreciate. She's bohemian in a town that can't spell the word—an artist, a kind artist—and people respond to her warmly, whereas I am kind, but people don't respond to me warmly. Except for the Hexagon. Without them, I'd probably be buried in a pile of newsprint and aluminum. Or still up a tree at the elementary school. No one will ever award me a Corn Dolly.

"Plenty of people think plenty of things when they see me, too," I say. "And then they get on the phone and call my dad and slam him for not parenting me very well. That's the way the world works, but are they right?"

She can't or won't answer the question. "I'm just . . . what if deep down Woods thinks I'm like my mom?"

Back to Woods. Back to dating. Still, I have an answer. "Then I'll kick his ass. But he doesn't."

In our history, Woods has never compared Janie Lee to her mother in the way she fears. Quite the opposite. I tell her this and she throws her leg over mine, snuggling up so close I smell the baking soda from her toothpaste.

"Billie?" Janie Lee's tone has the deep ring of a serious question. She feels along my arm. "That your elbow?"

"Yep."

Sliding her hand slowly down, she grips my fingers tight and solid. I wish I could see her eyes. They're gray, nearly clear, and sometimes they water when she's not crying. "You know what I told you the night of the fire?"

My heart is an assault rifle.

"How come you haven't said much about it?"

I taste blood.

"Did you hear me?" she asks.

Our faces are three inches apart. If I tip my forehead forward half an inch, I'll touch her glasses. "Billie? Don't fall asleep on me."

"I heard you," I admit.

"And?"

"I'm not sure how to feel." Like I wish we were still watching Betty White.

"Oh." She's worried.

Woods and Janie Lee make perfect sense in a photograph. But in real life? She's leaving at a sprint in "eleven months, eleven months," and he will commute to college and then die the mayor of Otters Holt, having never traveled elsewhere for more than a week. She's going to ruin the platonic ecosystem we have maintained in the Hexagon for years, for a relationship that will end in "eleven months, eleven months." Part of me wants to let this thing run its course, leave it uninterrupted. Because it will end. And then Woods will stay and I will return here after college. That's when we'll inevitably begin our us, and I'll call Janie Lee and say, "Woods and I . . . ," and she'll say, "I always knew you would."

None of these logical thoughts change the shouting match happening inside my head. She said she's in love. Is she? Am I? What does being in love mean? Surely, there is a spectrum of feelings between desire and love and being in love. Why is this not a class in high school?

Her voice interrupts. "I didn't think you'd be surprised."

"Did something happen between you two?" I dare to ask.

"We have this chemistry. It's there when we sing. I've tried turning it off, but then the night of the fire I was like, Why? Why would I turn this off? There's no one else like him. Except maybe you." Her stomach muscles contract in a giggle. She continues, "And sometimes I think about that silly wedding we did in third or fourth grade. You remember?"

Oh, yes. "I was his best man."

"What if that was a sign?"

"What if getting divorced the week after the wedding is the sign?" I ask.

She punches at me. The blow lands on my boob instead of my shoulder. "That was over tacos."

"I'm sure it's not the only divorce over tacos. Tacos are very important," I say flatly.

In this chess game, Janie Lee has her hand on my queen. It's nearly unbearable.

Several ticks of the clock later, she asks, "Should I tell him?"

I felt this question coming. Even though I could easily say no, no is the wrong answer for her to hear and me to give. No is selfish. I try to keep my selfishness on the inside, beating quietly like an organ that no one notices, a gallbladder, an appendix. "Probably," I say. "Maybe wait until after the Harvest Festival."

She makes a noise in the back of her throat as if this is unbearable. "So don't ask him to Sadie Hawkins?"

"I don't know."

There's another sigh. And then only white noise, of laundry tumbling round and round in the dryer, the dishwasher kicking to the next cycle, Dad humming a "How Great Thou Art" in his office. My eyes glaze over, fixing finally on the tiny green light of the fire alarm. It flashes every four seconds. I count ten flashes.

Janie Lee says, "I didn't want to tell you. It slipped out the night of the fire."

And I ask, "Why not?"

"I guess, well . . . I didn't want you to be afraid it would change us. We've been what we've been for so long I felt like I was cheating on you or something. That probably sounds weird, but you know what I mean? We're us." Without letting go of me, Janie Lee sets her glasses on my nightstand and snuggles closer. "We won't let anything ruin our us-ness, right? Because if it's him or you, well, no contest, my friend."

These words drip inside me. They touch my brain, my heart, my soul, my toes. I love her. Not for loving me. For loving us.

"Nothing," I promise.

Her lips or teeth always squeak when she wears a wide smile—I hear her squeaking. Less than a minute later, she snores as though all the problems in the world are solved.

For the first time since elementary school, I want to climb the great oak tree and never come down. Instead, I trace my thumb over the knuckle of her thumb in time with her breathing, and lie there. How long can I keep my world the way I want it?

When I'm sure I won't disturb her, I slide from the bed, into my boots, and down the hallway. Four of the five garage lights flicker to life. The one over Guinevere needs to be replaced; she's living in shadows.

"You and me both," I tell her, and set to work on the Daily Sit.

10

Davey's Part

A phone conversation between David Winters and Thomas Cahill on the night after Billie went to Nashville with Davey.

THOMAS: Spill. I know you need something. I felt a disruption in the universe.

DAVID: This is harder than I thought.

THOMAS: Which part?

DAVID: All of it.

THOMAS: All of it your granddad? All of it your dad? All of it Billie McCaffrey of Molly the Corn Dolly Otters Holt?

DAVID: A dreadful combination.

THOMAS: Unsurprising. So Billie is Daisy Mae?

DAVID: Billie is . . . complicated.

THOMAS: I'd say.

DAVID: You would?

THOMAS: Yes, because unless I'm wrong, Billie is very convinced we're together.

DAVID: Me and you?

THOMAS: You and me.

DAVID: Why?

THOMAS: David Winters, are you ashamed to be with me?

DAVID: Incredibly ashamed. Your body is stupid.

THOMAS: My body is a wonderland.

DAVID: I'm doubly ashamed now.

THOMAS: You wish you could get with me.

DAVID: I've been with you. Seventh grade. Your couch. World of Warcraft. Seventh grade. Environmental science class. Kayak number eight. Seventh—

THOMAS: Beside the point.

DAVID: The point exactly. We know what we look like when you're courting me—

THOMAS: I never courted, you antiquated fool.

DAVID: . . .

THOMAS: Okay, I courted you a little. I was quite young and rather ambitious.

DAVID: Regardless, we are NOT together now. And Gerry was. All. Over. You. Who wouldn't know you two were a couple?

THOMAS: Gerry was also all over Billie. Which, I must say, Billie did not mind.

DAVID: You'd never know if Billie minded. She's got a bajillion layers.

THOMAS: Well, one of those layers believes you're gay.

DAVID: Great. And another couple of them are maybe in love with two other people.

THOMAS: Two? She is also rather ambitious. Remind me to tell her not to kiss you in a kayak. Very unstable.

DAVID: You're giving me PTSD.

THOMAS: I kissed Gerry a bunch of times in front of her. Only as a sacrifice.

DAVID: I'm sure. What do you think makes her think we're together?

THOMAS: Well, we vibe. And in your I-do-not-have-to-please-John-Winters exploratory phase, perhaps she sees eyeliner and tight jeans and thinks gay. I assume metro isn't a look in Otters Holt.

DAVID: Not a popular one. Most of the dudes have a fish-hook on their person at all times. But eyeliner should not mean I want to sleep with you.

THOMAS: Blame the vibe.

DAVID: That damn vibe.

THOMAS: Gerry and I talked about it.

DAVID: The vibe?

THOMAS: No. You and Billie. We like her for you. And Gerry says she's grade-A in the kissing department.

DAVID: Well, thanks. Me too. But what should I do about the gay thing?

THOMAS: Well, you're not a hundred percent straight.

DAVID: I'm straight-ish. At the moment.

THOMAS: True. True. Plus, there's the problem of her liking two other people.

DAVID: I probably just need to let her think what she thinks.

THOMAS: If she thinks you're with me, she'll know you have excellent taste.

DAVID: Asshole.

THOMAS: You love me.

DAVID: I'd have to.

THOMAS: Seriously. Go with your gut on this thing. Tell her when it makes sense. Speaking of. What are you going to tell John Winters? She might be grade-A at kissing, but John will not find her fitting.

DAVID: He's been pressuring me.

THOMAS: About girls?

DAVID: No. About living with him.

THOMAS: You could be back by lacrosse season.

DAVID: I could.

THOMAS: You thinking about it?

DAVID: . . .

THOMAS: I interpret that silence to mean you really like Billie, eh?

DAVID: Yeah, but that's not it. I'm not sure what I'll do yet.

11

There's an after-church Hexagon meeting going on at Woods's house. A much-needed Save the Harvest Festival follow-up. I'm late. Dad needed an extra thirty minutes of my time.

"Billie," he said, waving me into his home office. I stood next to the coatrack, beside his robe, touching the velvet stole draped over the hanger. I've loved the feel of it since I spent Sunday mornings on his lap.

He whispered, "I've heard a rumor that your mother is on the Corn Dolly ballot this year."

I wondered who was telling him positive things. "That's great."

"Billie, this might really help us."

"I know."

Then came the ask. "Can you tread carefully?"

The thing is: my nose was clean. Serving old people, being nice, wearing a shirt that wasn't black to church this morning.

I promised him I would do my best.

He promised me that if Mom won a Corn Dolly no one would care about the fire.

We crossed our fingers that this rumor was correct. It was nice to be on his side again.

I push through the Carringtons' back door without a knock. The kitchen smells like peppermint tea, which makes me think of Big T. Mrs. Carrington clucks. "There's my favorite girl." She's standing at the counter, wearing yoga pants and a zippered fleece, attacking her grocery list. One of these days, if the festival doesn't die, she'll be awarded a Corn Dolly for being ungodly beautiful at fifty.

"Someone has to keep you on your toes," I tease, and steal an orange from the bowl.

She chews her pencil eraser, strains her ears toward the hallway. "They're in the game room. Try to make them behave."

"It'll take all five of them to make *me* behave, Mrs. C."

"Please. Your insides are all mushy and good."

"Take that back," I call over my shoulder.

I pause outside the game room door, anticipating the scene. Woods stands at the front of the room. Einstein is on his easel. Some action movie is reeling on the big screen, but everyone is watching Woods. Fifty, Janie Lee, Mash, and Davey—in that order—are sardines on the couch. There's a bowl of popcorn, two Mountain Dews, two waters, and Woods's mug of tea spread across the coffee table. Fifty's begging everyone to walk the beam; Woods is reminding them that "progress is imperative."

When I push open the door, I am correct in ninety-five percent of my prediction.

Post church, Woods has stripped to T-shirt and mesh shorts. He is twitchy with excitement and casting a forty-foot shadow over the entire room. I am overcome by the desire to tackle him straight on, tell the rest of these bastards to leave, and see if he'll watch the book television so I can nap on his shoulder. I wanted to be in a group, and now I want that group to be limited to two. Gerry said, *I don't kiss everyone. I kiss the people who have the little pieces of my soul.* I am struck again with the knowledge that Woods has one of my pieces.

Instead, I say, "You assholes started without me."

Woods throws a marker, which I catch and throw back. I launch the orange, too. It hits him in the chest and rolls under the couch. We'll find it in a year and blame the stain on Mash.

"We waited as long as we could," he says to me. To Davey, he says, "Elizabeth who?"

Davey drums his fingers on the side table. They nearly blur. And that's just like him. He's a helicopter. He could lift off, right here, and I wouldn't be surprised. Catching my eye, he halts his fingers, looks at me, warns me about something without saying a word.

Unfazed, I give him the standard up-nod, and vault over

the back of the couch. After having stepped on nearly every-one, I settle on the floor directly in front of Mash.

"If you throw up on me, I'll never forgive you," I say, and pull his leg hair. "What's going on?"

Mash's face is redder than the radishes in Grandy's garden. He has a smattering of freckles over the bridge of his nose that look like sprinkles on a cupcake. They make him look inno-cent. His blush makes him appear guilty. "Einstein is currently rescuing our love lives."

"It's going to take more than Einstein to do that," I tell them. "We can blow up a sock and burn down a church, but limitations, people, limitations. I thought we were brainstorm-ing KickFall and fund-raising."

I've thrown off Woods's ju-ju with my negativity and he has to refocus. "We are. But delay of game. You, Billie McCaffrey . . . are just in time to . . . help us . . . figure out the Sadie Hawkins part of Harvest Festival." Every pause, he adds some unseen stroke to Einstein. Every stroke, my stom-ach knots.

"That sounds like a terrible way to spend a Sunday after-noon," I say.

Last year, the dance flew under our radar. We watched the Corn Dolly competition—a token year, the Corn Dolly was given posthumously to Reagan Gentry, our Spanish teacher, who died of a brain aneurysm—and then square-danced our asses off in a large group. I didn't think it was strange that we were the only people our ages not looking for a corner away from the watchful eyes of adults. I thought it was marvelous.

"But the girls ask the guys."

Leave it to Fifty to state the obvious.

"That means four out of six people in this room have no say," I tell Fifty, peering around Woods's body to read Einstein. Only the top of the board is visible. "'The Hexagon of Love,'" I read. "The whole thing is a little pretentious. Couldn't we just go for the standard love triangle?"

No one is listening. This happens when Woods is in full swing.

"Elizabeth Rawlings is an interesting choice," he says to Davey.

Elizabeth Rawlings is a junior with a good first name, a bent for Sylvia Plath, and the most perfectly straight teeth God ever made. We were on the softball team in middle school. She bounced around through various groups and wound up being one of those tights and cat T-shirt girls. She's probably biding her time in Otters Holt, dreaming of a commune in California. Is this who Davey believes is his equal? I reject the idea.

Her friends call her Lizzie. This has always been a point of consideration for me. There are many ways to shorten our name—Liz, Lizzie, Libby, Lib, Beth, Betsy, Liza—none of which I tolerate. I can't imagine being a Lib. I'd rather run naked off Rock Quarry Cliff or fall off Vilmer's Beam.

Mash gives a half laugh at the board and at me. Maybe he's surprised at his cousin's choice. Maybe he's just glad I'm here. I too am slightly surprised Davey hasn't named Thomas, and

I'm not the only one. Fifty mouths "Audi Thomas" to me. He stops smiling when I flip him off.

Despite Fifty's comment, Davey could come out to this group if he wanted to. None of *us* would flip our shit. Especially not Janie Lee and me. We've heard it all. Two inseparable girls: must be gay. *I saw them holding hands. One of them is dykeish. They cooed at each other when they were reading* Romeo and Juliet.

There are a few students at school who are out. Not an easy path. Most people wait until college, and then move to bigger cities. The price of their sexual freedom is paid for with a loss of home, and often a loss of community respect. In 2005, a beloved woman in town, Corn Dolly winner 1984, married her girlfriend, whom everyone had thought was her roommate, in Canada. The committee didn't ask for her Dolly back, but they "accidentally" printed the calendar without her name in 2006. This is the kind of thing you don't forget. It's the kind of thing that makes you want to control the Corn Dolly committee. The kind of thing that makes you want to override the system.

I'd like to believe my generation is different. We'd give a Corn Dolly to a gay woman. We've all read enough, watched enough, YouTubed enough to understand sexuality isn't black and white. What do we care who someone finds attractive or falls in love with? But that doesn't mean you don't need a machete and some body armor if you want to walk the openly gay road in Otters Holt.

Dad is always up my ass about wearing jeans and muscle

shirts. And it's not because he's worried about skin cancer on my arms. "Billie, people think where there's smoke there's fire."

If Davey went openly gay, I can predict the consequences the way I predicted the state of this room when I arrived. My dad would reread his youth ministry textbooks on *Generation Z and Sexuality* and *Raising Conservative Teens in a Liberal World*. People would wear oven mitts to handle him. They'd say, "I should have known. Did you see his eyeliner?" Girls my age would say, "It's a shame" or "I wonder if he's bi." Who knows how his parents would feel, but they would certainly have opinions.

Elizabeth Rawlings is a safe choice, but Davey's never struck me as someone dedicated to safety.

"Doesn't Elizabeth Rawlings draw pentagrams on all her notebooks?" Fifty asks.

"Why aren't we doing something fun?" I ask in return. "This is lame."

Davey pulls a pillow into his lap and goes back to his drumming. "We're not allowed. Woods decided we have to lose our man-cards by charting out the dance."

His expression says: *We should be in your garage.*

Mine says: *Let's blow this pop stand.*

Against better judgment, we both stay put.

"So let me get this straight. You five are trying to figure out how to get dates?"

Five noses scrunch. Five semi-nods. My disapproval is so visible, Fifty lands the lowest of blows.

"You look like your dad."

"Oooooohhhh," Woods and Janie Lee say together. Each watches my response.

"Good thing I'm against murder on the Sabbath," I tell Fifty.

"I'm terrified," he says.

Fifty and I are two Betta fish in the same tank. Eventually, I'm going to eat him. But for now, it's easier to join the chaos. There's history between us. Dance history. Sadie Hawkins is held outdoors in the middle of town if it isn't raining, in Vilmer's Barn if it is. Eighth grade, Fifty and I did some very G-rated experimenting and missed the whole dang Corn Dolly presentation and half the dance. That was the year Mash's mama, Jeanelle, won. 2013. Fifty and I never told a soul we missed it. We certainly wouldn't tell them why. For an asshat, he's got the softest lips.

"All right, deal me in," I say.

Davey says, very matter-of-factly, "Just remember this Hexagon of Love all started with Woods."

"It started with wood all right," I joke.

This is not the first time anyone has made a Woods's wood joke. We land on familiar ground. Everyone cackles except Woods, who isn't laughing because he's too busy lunging at me. He's twice my weight, so when he drags me into the middle of the floor and draws dry-erase lines down my nose and across my cheeks, I am forced to jab his ribs incessantly like a child. "If you break my sunglasses—" I threaten.

He's squirming and nearly defeated when Mash says, "Better not let Mary Dancy see you mounting Billie like that."

From beneath the attack, I say, "Mary Dancy?" very differently from the other three boys chanting, "Mary Dancy, Mary Dancy, Mary Dancy."

In a quick, painful, show-stopping moment, I get my first look at the top of Einstein—a line attaches Woods Carrington to Mary Dancy. Janie Lee throws an UGG at Woods's head—the first good use of those boots.

Breathless, I cock my head to the side. Reread. Mary Dancy? She's the only female in the history of Otters Holt who has ever kicked for the football team. She has rock-hard quads *and* a stack of tiaras from the county fair and a zillion other beauty contests.

It all started with Woods, Davey had said.

"What do you two think?" Woods directs his question at Janie Lee and me.

I *think* my eyes might explode and take Janie Lee's heart along in the explosion.

I say, "I'm forming an opinion."

"Me too," Janie Lee chirps.

Sadie fucking Hawkins.

Everyone hee-haws at something Fifty says and none of them, except Davey, hears me ask, "Am I on the board?"

Davey tightens the laces on his high tops, throws me sympathy from the corner of his eye. Woods moves aside. I read the whole board.

HEXAGON OF LOVE

GUYS   GIRLS

WOODS _____ MARY DANCY
MASH
FIFTY _____ CARLEY DAVIS
DAVEY _____ ELIZABETH RAWLINGS
  ?   JANIE LEE
BILLIE   ?

12

I read the board again. Guys = Mash, Woods, Fifty, Davey, and *Billie.*

I am not waffling on my tombstone inscription. *Elizabeth McCaffrey, born 1999—d. ? IN LOVING MEMORY: She had balls.*

This is not conjecture, because when I say, "WTF?" to the whole lot of them, Fifty says, "You got the biggest balls in the room, B," and Woods adds, "Yours dropped before Mash's," and then Mash salutes my nonexistent balls.

Which leaves me grasping at Janie Lee, who was, I might add, sharing a twin bed with me on the night I got my period in seventh grade. Among the Hexagon, she is the one person who should be saying, *Hold up a minute.*

Here's the problem: Janie Lee's not a boat rocker. If Woods Carrington wrote FIVE WAYS TO KILL PUPPIES on Einstein, she'd endure and cry like a fountain when she got home. Her tongue is currently lodged in her yellow-bellied gut, and mine is fixed to the roof of my mouth.

Davey appears nine kinds of torn. Part of him wants to punch Woods and Fifty in the face. Part of him wants to text Audi Thomas to escape this meeting. Instead, he drums, his nails galloping against the table like horses running on asphalt. Over and over, he drums.

Behind me, Mash chokes on a peanut and throws up on the other side of the couch.

"*Seriously*, dude," Woods says, as if he is surprised.

Mash has throw-up tears rolling down his cheeks. "Sorry, guys."

Like clockwork, Mrs. C appears in the doorway—the sound of Mash's hurling is a very specific thing—and sets a towel and some carpet cleaner on the closest table. She pats the items as if they are friends and tells her son, "Don't let it sit. I'm off to the grocery."

Woods and Mash cleaning up puke gives me two minutes to think.

Here are the facts:

I'm no stranger to dyke comments.

I'm a thorn, not a petal.

If *Playboy* did a spread on flat-chested women, I'd be a cover model.

And not a single one of those things mattered, ever, not even when I was quizzed on sexuality by my own pastor father, until put into a different context by the Hexagon. Does Woods, master of the marker, think I'm gay? Or is he like, "Billie's my brother?" or "Billie wishes she were Bill." Or maybe being gay is synonymous with being a tomboy to them? I am baffled.

Woods is returning from the bathroom; he's offering Mash a glass of water, all while I'm making up my mind about tackling this situation. There's only one thing to do right now that does not involve me crying and screaming: go with it.

"If you leave me there, you'll have to retool Einstein to say WAYS FOR BILLIE TO FIND A NEW HOME. Brother Scott would flip," I say.

Davey's galloping fingers stop. He gives me the briefest headshake as Fifty and Mash clap and catcall. He realizes I've chosen to soldier on. Two people in this room usually read my mind, and both of them missed my sexuality or gender or both by a mile.

It's a lot to process and hide. Even for me.

Mash has a thought. "I'm not sure it's wise to blow up a microwave and date a girl in the same month. But if anyone can do it, you can."

One vote for gay.

Woods sashays over and scrubs the top of my head. "Billie doesn't let anyone tell her what to do. Not even Brother Scott. Right, B?"

This earns him a hearty nod, even though I'm currently letting five jerkoffs tell me exactly what to do. In my head, I stand and scream, "Raise your hand if you have a vagina and you're not gay." In actuality, I bite the insides of my cheek and freeze my face in a blank stare.

Meanwhile, Janie Lee stops rubbing Mash's arm—I assume she decides he has the peanut problem under control—and slides onto the floor next to me. She leans her head on my shoulder. It's awkward for me, but I pat her hair—the way I would a puppy. Her hot cheek presses against my shoulder, her pain presses against my anger. I suppose she's having a crisis too. Janie Lee loves Woods, who likes Mary dang Dancy. And I like him, and I've thought about liking her, and they've thought about me having a dick.

In an epic gesture, Woods sweeps his hand in front of both columns on the board and asks me, "Well, what think ye, Billie McCaffrey?"

Now, I've been known to hate on my father, but I silently worship at the altar of his teachings. *Billie, don't ever let them see you tremble. The church eats the trembling man.* I go toe-to-toe. "I think Clyde Lacken will kick your overly presumptuous ass if you make a move on Mary. And I want to know why Mash is holding out."

Mash musses Janie Lee's hair. "J-Mill is all mum and shit too. Pick on her."

Fifty says, "Mash, go on and admit to us what you've been admitting in your shower for years: you're in love with yourself."

Woods will stomach the occasional sex joke, but he's old-fashioned enough that he'd rather avoid a full-blown masturbation conversation when his mother could still be in hearing distance. "You don't have to pick anyone," he tells Mash. "But you"—he stares at Janie Lee with great persuasion in his chocolate eyes—"must."

Janie Lee turns her gaze on me and says ten boat-rocking words. "What if I wanted to choose someone in this room?"

This is how really bad becomes terrible. I teleport into her brain and scream: Don't do it, Miller.

She hears me, ignores every word.

The whole room tilts as if we're on a ride at the county fair. That doesn't keep Woods from stating, "By ordinance of the Great Christmas Dance Debacle of 2012, I feel obligated to remind you that we have a code."

He's referring to the finger cutting and blood-oath swearing we did following the Great Christmas Dance Debacle of 2012: *I, Billie McCaffrey am platonically in love with the following: Woods Carrington, Kevin "Mash" Vilmer, Robert "Fifty" Tilghman, and Janie Lee Miller. I swear to honor group above self unless I am in love with one of the aforementioned, in which case, I may pursue my individual desires.* (Woods had spent the previous summer reading the complete works of Jane Austen and John Grisham.) As a pack of sexually innocent puppies, we've obeyed every ordinance. Until now.

Everyone except me wants to know who Janie Lee is considering. There's not a person in the room who wouldn't date her.

She makes a fist, presses it into her quad. "Oh, screw the code."

Fifty sinks his teeth into the bone. "Now you have to tell us, Miller."

She speaks, voice rattling like coffee beans in a can. "Maybe I'm not even breaking the code. Maybe . . . well, maybe I'm saying I'm . . . in love with one of you."

I find her hand in mine when it wasn't there before. The four boys stare. To hell with them. I squeeze her fingers between mine and beg her not to go this route. *Don't tell them about Woods. Don't tell them about Woods. There's no going back from that.*

Woods drops his marker and it rolls across the carpet toward me.

"Billie? Janie Lee? What's going on?"

"Nothing," I answer Woods. "Nothing at all."

"We've talked about this," Janie Lee says to me.

She's asking permission, which is ridiculous, and we've got so much lesbian ambience going on right now the boys are currently having a fantasy about the two of us in my twin bed. Fifty whistles to that effect.

Davey throws advice at Woods. "Drop it, why don't you?"

Woods Carrington never dropped a thing in his life. "Janie Lee?" he asks.

She stalls momentarily. "Well, the dance. All I'm asking is, what if I wanted to go with one of you?" Her eyes scan the room, landing on four other pairs of eyes; her thumb moves absent-mindedly back and forth over the pulse in my wrist. "Could we amend the code slightly?" She asks this question of Woods.

"Depends on which one of us it is," Fifty answers straightaway.

"Shut *up*, Fifty," Woods says.

Woods touches Einstein, as if connection with the board will settle him. Losing control of the peanut gallery wasn't on his agenda when he led this discussion toward the Harvest Festival. Rather than answer, he says to me, "I need to see you in the next room."

I release myself from Janie Lee's clutches and follow him into the bathroom off the hall. We hear Fifty say, "*Mom and Dad* are fighting."

The toilet seat is up. I'm tempted to tell Woods, *Hang on a minute while I unzip my fly and take a piss.* It's a good thing I don't, because he wraps his arms around me so tightly I lose my breath. Our hearts race against each other.

"You going to save this one, Einstein?" I whisper into the crease lines of his T-shirt.

He collapses onto the edge of the tub. "Tell me what's going on," he says from behind a mask of his hands.

I put on my guessing cap. He thinks Janie Lee is in love with me, and I'm in love with her, and no one told him. He wants an apology. We are best friends. I lean against the vanity. "I think you're probably experiencing what we mortals call jealousy."

"Maybe I am," he says.

I did not expect to be right. I said it to say something.

He makes himself ask the question he doesn't want to ask. "Are you two . . . together?"

It is neither wise nor prudent to let the guy I *love* believe I'm *in love* with the girl who is actually, maybe, *in love* with him, but the words that come from my mouth are these: "I'm not sure what we are."

I find . . . I am not lying.

Feelings don't sort like laundry.

Woods needs all his people in neat little boxes with neat little labels. He needs me to be his *best* friend. He *needs* for Janie Lee, Mash, Fifty, and Davey to be *the* Hexagon. He needs assurances. In the church, even if people are one thing, they are often another. Brother Scott taught me that even if people *are* boxes, they are boxes on a Rubik's Cube that shift. One turn, one conversation, one thought—all shift the cube.

I've loved Woods for so long, but Janie Lee . . . maybe it's time to stop and define my feelings. I was always too busy insisting and explaining that Janie Lee and I weren't together and it was no one's business and "please stop making assumptions," that I never stopped to consider that we *are* in a unique relationship. I suddenly feel as if I've owned a castle for years and explored only one room. Janie Lee's good people. No, she's best people. It's ridiculous not to consider her . . . and the board, oddly enough, gave me the anger to understand I have more choices than I realized.

Woods says, "Jesus, Billie."

"Oh, I don't think Jesus is involved in this one yet."

Woods forces himself to say each word thoughtfully, carefully, without judgment. "You two have always had a thing, a connection that's different than with the rest of us, but I didn't realize it was . . . something. I thought it was because you're both girls."

It takes everything in my power to respond with, "It's not like that," instead of *Oh, am I a girl now?*

I'm not sure he believes me. He lifts his head. "Regardless, how do we proceed from here?"

I love him so dearly for that *we*.

"We go back in there and you erase the board and write WAYS TO CHANGE THE WORLD or ODD USES FOR PEANUT BUTTER or FIVE THINGS MASH WILL CHOKE ON BY MAY, and act like you're Woods effing Carrington."

"I'm a little off my game," he admits.

I have his dry-erase marker in my pocket. I turn his palm up. I write *President* on one hand and *Commander* on the other, and say, "Walk into that game room and act like the Hexagon of Love never happened. And let people work out Sadie Hawkins on their own."

He head-bobs. He stands. We're due another crushing hug, but instead he grabs my head like a basketball and tilts my forehead toward his mouth. His lips are above my right eyebrow. They are silk.

"Forgive me." His mouth tickles my forehead.

Woods only likes change he creates, but he owns his mistakes.

"We'll talk it through," I promise. And add, "After you fix that mess in there. Go be Dad."

He chews the side of his thumbnail, lingers long enough to say, "Meet me on the roof tonight for Beggar." Without waiting for my answer, he returns to the game room. His voice calls out in its usual commanding way, "Gather round, my children. New plan."

I don't have to peek around the door to know Einstein now says something ostentatious in Woods's impeccable handwriting. Or to know that everyone in that room follows him to a new topic the way they'd follow him through the gates of hell.

13

Action heroes have at least three ways of being shot. Hero One: takes a single bullet to the wrong location and goes down fast with no last words. Hero Two: takes an uncountable amount of lead to vital organs, stays upright long enough to save someone, falls bravely. Hero Three: takes an entire .45 clip to the brain, stumbles off camera, and everyone knows she'll be back.

I am Hero Three.

And Hero Three is currently sitting on the freezer in her garage pulling lead out of her brain and figuring out how to build a better couch. The Daily Sit is uncooperative, which is in keeping with its ornery personality. Despite this, I love the Daily Sit fiercely. I need the distraction.

Last night Janie Lee and I walked to the Fork and Spoon

after the failed Hexagon meeting. She cried into her milk shake (and then mine), and I made her go home and play her violin to me over the phone until she calmed down. She felt terrible about the whole not-standing-up-for-my-vagina thing, and I felt terrible for suggesting she silence her desires for Woods.

We'll recover. The only real fights we've ever had—ones in which we didn't speak for multiple hours—were over Green Day being sellouts, and *Star Wars* episodes I to III. This wasn't a fight. But it is something that will weasel its way into future arguments.

How could you be so selfish? future Janie Lee might ask.

You know, I was thinking the same thing when you let Woods put me on the guys' side of the Hexagon board, future Billie might respond.

You're the one who held me back from Woods. You're the reason we aren't together, future Janie Lee would yell back.

Yeah, well, maybe you're not supposed to be with him. Maybe you're supposed to be with me. I wouldn't have yelled that part, but I would have thought it.

Friendship relies on history—on history being positive even when it's painful. I have to find a way to erase last night the way Woods erases Einstein. I am not sure how. So while the Hexagon is at school, I'm taking a mental health day. Neither Mom nor Dad questioned my "migraine." The moment Dad left for visitation ministry, Mom retreated to her studio, and I parked myself in the garage to think about the fact that I had two meet-ups last night. The one with Janie Lee. The one after Janie Lee fell asleep on the phone.

I arrived at the elementary school before Woods.

Rusted playground equipment rose out of the scattered pea gravel like a metal graveyard. I squinted at the run-down ball field, where we will hold the KickFall tournament. The grass in the outfield was the shin height of a giant.

I shimmied up a triangular-shaped antenna fastened to the school building with some luck and eroded hinges. The rungs were familiar with my weight and didn't complain in the least. When I stepped out onto the roof, heat from the day, trapped in the tar-like substance, pressed into the rubber of my tennis shoes. I was sweaty from biking over, but the extra heat was pleasant against the chill.

While waiting for Woods, I stared at the tiny metropolis of Otters Holt: the token caution light, miles and miles of electrical transmission towers pulling power from Kentucky Dam, and the massive dark caverns of the limestone quarry. Power and darkness were everywhere. The evening was quiet except for a barking dog and the Vilmers' bleating goats. Otters Holt by night was all ghost, no town. The elementary school beneath me needed every ounce of love we planned to show it now that youth group community service was slowing down.

Woods was stepping off the antenna—a fact I was ignoring–not ignoring. He loped toward me, jacket draped over his arm. "Thought you might be cold," he said. The silky fabric of his favorite windbreaker landed on my shoulders. He hugged me from behind, leaving his arms in a knot around my chest. Leaving my heart in a knot.

"You think Hattie is feeding those goats?" he asked.

"Do you really have to feed goats?" I asked.

We lifted our shoulders in unison. He was a full head taller than me and always had been. When we stood this way, I was eight years old again, with a spray of freckles, bowl-cut hair, and pockets filled with fossils and special rocks. Back then, Woods wrote sloppy lists on his Dad's yellow legal pads. They said FOUR THINGS BETTER THAN COTTON CANDY and IF SANTA WERE PRESIDENT OF OUR CLASS and POP ROCKS PLUS VINEGAR AND STUFF.

"Van Gogh would be inspired by this view," he said, his lips nearly against my ear. "Paint me something that looks like this for when we're old."

Seventeen-year-old me returned.

Woods Carrington always smelled either like he needed a shower or he'd just toweled off. Oatmeal and honey oozed from his pores. He must have "forgotten" again to tell his mother to get his manly-man shampoo at BI-LO, and he'd showered in her bathroom. I wanted to eat him. Instead, I bumped my head against his chin, told him he was right about Van Gogh, and mentioned the shower. He confessed that he might just be a honey and oatmeal guy. We rocked, left, right, left, sharing balance, neither of us eager to break apart.

"And you are a"—he smelled my hair—"hayfield and epoxy girl."

Elizabeth McCaffrey, born 1999—d. ? IN LOVING MEMORY: a hayfield and epoxy girl.

"Let's play Beggar," I said.

We claimed a corner of the roof where the old gym slopes to meet the lower cafeteria wall. It was a cave cut from brick and glass, sitting well beyond the range of Mrs. John's security light across the street. We opened a ragtag deck of cards, and Woods's fingers moved nimbly over them, the cards singing as they slapped against the old cooler we keep on the roof for a table.

The wind lifted his cowlick, teasing hair that was usually contained by a baseball cap. His hair was the one disorderly thing about him. Everything else could be described as neat-as-a-pin, an item on a list, well-ordered. I was glad he hadn't worn the cap. He looked boyish in it, and I needed to remember we were not eight.

"Let's build a house up here and never move," he said after the cards were dealt.

"Only if you buy us a dragon," I said.

He grinned as if he knew a guy with dragon eggs, and I'd better want what I'd asked for. That was where I'd gotten into trouble with him. Woods and I had never had many *things* in common. He was music, and I was sports. He was peppermint tea, and I was an energy drink. He was class president, and I was named an "Art Alien" by an underground school blog. But we lived life on the same frequency, leading and striving and wanting. Inside both of us lurked someone young and someone ancient.

"What are you thinking about?" he asked.

I answered, "Love," and he scrunched his nose appropriately.

"What'd you wanna go and do that for?" he asked.

I said, "I needed a word for my favorite card game."

I thought, *Because of your damn whiteboard, Hexagon bullshit.*

He swatted at my cards, laughing.

Beggar is a game we learned on a youth ski trip, and while the others abhorred it, Woods and I wasted centuries on the rooftop with a deck of cards and a game of luck. I rarely won. Woods maintained I was secretly competitive, which drove me crazy. I wasn't nearly as competitive as all the guys believed. I was just good at stuff they didn't expect girls to be good at.

He dealt, and we played.

He won four straight games.

"Tell me everything you're thinking," he said, when I threw my cards atop the cooler.

He rested his weight on his palms, leaning away from me for the first time that night.

I began. "One. Other than my imaginary gigantic balls, I don't understand why you put me on the guys' side of the board. Two. Other than your imaginary gigantic balls, I don't understand why you put Mary Dancy on the board at all. You don't even know her. Three. When I said I don't know how I feel about Janie Lee, I meant it. Four. The real messy awkward truth is . . ." He prepared himself by affixing his gaze to Mrs. John's front porch. "Honestly, I always thought . . . well, I always thought . . . *we'd give it a go.*"

He said two barely audible words. "Me too."

I was prepared for *Billie, we can't,* or *Billie, I'm sorry,* or *Billie, you're like a brother to me.* Nothing in my emotional response arsenal went with *Me too.*

I said, "I guess I always thought it worked like this. You talk. You kiss. You fall in love, buy a Buick, and never leave Otters Holt. There's sex in there somewhere."

"Me too. Except the Buick. We can do better than a Buick."

At that precise moment, the wide neck of my sweatshirt had fallen off my shoulder, and he stared at my naked collarbone. Under his lingering gaze, I did not doubt he knew that I was made of girl. I righted the fabric, and he trapped my hand with his. "B, there's a lot of people I love, but there's no one like you."

Exposed skin will do that.

My brain crunched thoughts so loudly it sounded as if I were snacking on Doritos. "What does that mean?" I asked.

"I don't like Mary Dancy," he said.

"But you're attracted to Janie Lee," I argue.

"And so are you, but that doesn't change this. Us."

When we were younger, I tried to teach Janie Lee and

Woods how to make friendship bracelets from cross-stitch thread. Each bracelet was made up of a certain number of strands, a certain pattern of cinching knots against each other. This was friendship. We were four strands. Then five strands. Six strands now. And a series of knots, all in neat little rows, made up our history. I had always thought, always believed, we would stick to that design and I would know the future, because I knew the pattern.

Woods was untying a knot. The pattern was changing.

He touched the small of my back, beneath my sweatshirt. His fingers brushed the recessed place at the bottom of my spine. "You have to know that you're my second skin." His thumb moved like a metronome.

"And who is Janie Lee to you?"

He spoke, and as he did, I said the word with him. "Music."

Music in the way she moved, music in the way she spoke, music in the way she listened. She was a melody we both hummed.

He breathed on my chin, my cheek, my neck. His teeth were so near my earlobe I heard his breath inside my chest. "What do we do with all this love?" he asked.

"I don't know," I said. Gerry had kissed me, and we'd been fine afterward. Perhaps we were holding our relationship like crystal and it was one of those pink bouncy balls. "Maybe you should kiss us both and see how you feel."

He didn't laugh.

I thought I would be nervous.

I thought it would be a big deal.

I thought Saturn might fall out of the sky and cause a tsunami on the other side of the planet.

But when he kissed me, and I kissed him (and I feel like I have to say it exactly that way because it was equal), we were what we'd always been: friends.

I'd really only kissed four people at that point: Fifty, Renley (who moved away freshman year), Gerry, and now Woods. But it was enough to compare. Kissing Woods made me want to say, "If we haven't found someone we're in love with by the time we're forty, let's get married," or "Let's be each other's backup plan." Because he was someone I would marry and raise dragons with and let cut my yellow toenails at seventy, but he wasn't . . . Well, he wasn't even Gerry.

Elizabeth McCaffrey, born 1999—d. ? R.I.P.: She never bought a Buick.

I know passion isn't everything, and relationships aren't just physical, blah, blah, blah, but we were perfunctory. Shockingly perfunctory. And hiding seventeen years' worth of collapsed desire took all my energy.

"That was nice," he said, lips hovering inches above mine. And then he kissed me a second time as if the first hadn't quite convinced him.

I felt polite.

"Yes, that was very nice," I said when it was over.

We both wiped our mouths with our sleeves.

I used my poker face, I used my sweet voice, I embellished. "If Janie Lee kisses like that, we're all really going to have a problem," I told him.

Because it was one thing to tease him about his imaginary gigantic balls, but it was quite another to deflate them.

THE SHORT PART
before
PART TWO

*The degree to which a person can grow is directly
proportional to the amount of truth he can accept about
himself without running away.*
—LELAND VAL VAN DE WALL

FIVE YEARS EARLIER

The rock ledge felt cool and slippery to Janie Lee's bare feet. She stood nearly thirty feet off the water, an eternity. Summer sun blazing down, turning skin from pale to olive. She looked down, down, down—her knees knocking, her heart fluttering. Heights: they weren't friends. They'd been forced into acquaintance two weeks before.

For reasons she understood but detested, her classmates had adopted jumping off Rock Quarry Cliffs as gospel fun. She blamed puberty. The boys had been more annoying lately: jumping off things, hitting on others, making stupid dares.

They ran right off the cliffs like their asses were on fire. To Janie Lee, it was one thing to risk a walk across Vilmer's Beam and fall into a pile of hay. Another to smack into the lake's liquid concrete. She wasn't scared of dying—hundreds, perhaps thousands, had made this jump; she just didn't appreciate senseless pain. But she was faced with a new decision. The pain of red, smacked flesh or of red, smacked loneliness? She knew the answer.

As so, she had docked her uncle's johnboat, climbed and switched back over slippery rocks holding on to a green-knotted rope, and scrambled over spray-painted messages from hundreds of jumpers to stand atop Rock Quarry Cliff. To hopefully find someone to eat lunch with this year.

One false start, one running attempt, one set of windmilling arms: she was falling.

Her stomach and throat connected. Her heart thundered in her ears. She sliced through the water without a scream, proud as a peacock.

Cold water streamed up her nose; something grazed her leg. She kicked out and up, racing toward oxygen. Swimming in Kentucky Lake meant sharing this gigantic pool with fish. Only she hadn't kicked a fish, and the sting in her upper thigh wasn't from entering the water wrong.

She'd landed on a water moccasin that did not appreciate being kicked.

Swelling, nausea, throbbing. All at once. Pain tied her like a dock rope. She clawed her way to the surface.

In the next cove, Billie McCaffrey baited a hook and asked her father, "Did you hear that?" Her dad was listening to headphones and hadn't heard anything. She pulled the earpiece away, and said, "Anchor up. Drive to the cliffs."

Janie Lee's right leg was already a heavy, useless appendage. By then she'd pieced together that there was poison in her bloodstream, spidering its way up to her heart. By then she'd pieced together that she could die.

She was thinking about God. Wondering if there were violins in Heaven.

She was not thinking about Billie McCaffrey, even though she had often thought of Billie McCaffrey, until she and her dad showed up and hauled a nearly unconscious Janie Lee into their boat.

They were front-page news: Minister's Daughter Dives into Snake-Infested Water to Save Best Friend.

The paper declared them best friends, and it was so.

Janie Lee gained momentary hero status at school and the instant affection of Woods, Mash, and Fifty. A group of four became a group of five, and Billie McCaffrey made true and dear friends with a girl. They'd been nod-at-each-other classmates before—now they were magnetized. Two town daughters—one the boyish offspring of a local minister, and the other the daughter of a drug dealer—fell into cahoots.

Some people said they fell in love.

Some people were always making assumptions.

PART TWO

EINSTEIN WAS AN IDIOT

There are chapters in every life which are seldom read
and certainly not aloud.
—CAROL SHIELDS

14

The Saturday morning the Corn Dolly ballot is due for release, Woods and I are on his bed, heads touching, watching the book television. A much-needed break. At his prompting, we pulled double duty this week. Community service projects *and* the painstaking process of clearing unwanted things from the elementary school lot. Save the Harvest Festival is alive and well, and so far it's making me want to wallow in a vat of Icy Hot and sleep for a year.

All week we met at 6:45 and worked for a solid hour before school. "Chop. Chop. Get her done," chirped Woods, the happy overlord. Post-school, we went to our assigned senior citizens. I've reroofed a shed, I've painted a bathroom the color of lilacs, I've made approximately four million trips to Goodwill and three to the dump. Yay for dirty, sweaty redemption. I am behind on homework, have eaten a dozen homemade cookies, and have ignored the mysteries of kissing altogether. Yay for dirty, sweaty distractions.

I was too bone-tired to stand over the Daily Sit and glue another damn anything to anything. So when Woods texted, and didn't want nothing other than company, I biked over. I noted that he was very clear about "not wanting nothing other than company."

His mom vacuums in the hallway. I wish she'd suck up our impatience. The newspaper should be out already. Woods has already trekked to the Fork and Spoon and claims there is nothing to report.

"What did they make you sing?" I ask.

He groans. "Elvis."

"Glad I didn't get up for that."

"Whatever. You get up with the sun."

Fable. The sun is not involved. If I go to bed at one, I'll wake up at six. Thus far, five hours is my limit. Before anyone else in my house woke, I spent three hours on the Daily Sit. To no avail. "Do you know how many layers of newspaper it takes to make something the depth of a couch?" I complain.

"I'm sure you're counting."

I was. But Davey added some layers when I was in the shower, and accuracy went out the window.

"That reminds me." Woods retrieves his keys from his pocket, drops them on my stomach. "Grandy sent you her news-papers. And some aluminum cans. They're all in my trunk."

I drop the keys on his crotch. "On my bike, genius. You'll have to drop them off later."

We watch the book television some more. Woods changes the channel three times, lands on a cartoon. Mrs. Carrington finally stops vacuuming and starts clanking in the kitchen. I'm massaging my own shoulders thinking I'll never finish anything. Woods has two vertical worry lines stretching from his eyebrows to his hairline. These occur every time he focuses on stuff he can't control.

Is he thinking about me? Is he thinking about how terrible our kissing attempt was?

In an alt-universe, where Janie Lee said nothing the night of the fire, we would continue through graduation in normalcy. A single sentence set us on a course of redefinition, of pairs, of *benefits*. Benefits were always my lowest frequency setting. Now I think about them, well . . . frequently. And I think about them with everyone. Even Fifty. I want to Dial-soap my brain.

Woods has no upper lip to speak of. Why do I know that? Because I'm staring at his mouth.

His mouth is forming sentences about the Harvest Festival, KickFall, and the Corn Dolly nominations.

"Who do you think will make the ballot?" he asks.

I draw a large, ironic heart shape in the air with my fingers. "Tawny, of course."

"Obviously. But who else?"

"There's not a woman in Otters Holt who wouldn't be happy to win the Corn Dolly. Especially if it's the last one."

"Oh, it ain't over. Not by a long shot."

There's such a fine line between things Woods plans to do and things Woods has done that he assumes we've already saved the festival, even if no one comes out for KickFall.

Woods props himself up on an elbow, pulls at a loose thread on his comforter. "What about you? You want a Corn Dolly?"

"No," I say quickly. I love the Corn Dolly and what it represents in Otters Holt, but I would never pursue one.

I was seven, maybe eight. I'd seen an old movie—*The NeverEnding Story*—and as I was prone to do at the time, I obsessed over the main character. Who went on adventures. Who flew on luck dragons. Who faced shit down like a pro. Following Wednesday-night church, I marched myself into the bathroom with scissors and gave myself a haircut that resembled the main character's. Nearly a foot of dark hair was on the tile floor.

Dad found me. He must have said something like, *Elizabeth, what have you done?* And I must have said, *Daddy, I'm Atreyu.* Those words are hazy, but I do remember the words that followed: "Elizabeth, Atreyu is a boy. You are a girl."

And I didn't understand what he meant, only that it sounded like girls couldn't go on adventures. He dragged me kicking and screaming from the bathroom to my mother. And while I sat, calming myself on her lap, a lady, maybe Tawny or someone else, said, "Well, that one will never win a Corn Dolly."

I've known this all my life. Internalized it. And everyone else has too.

"Oh, come on." He digs his chin into my chest until I cough.

I palm his head to stop him. "I'm serious. But I'd love to see my mom or Janie Lee on the ballot someday. I think they are both that invisible sort of good, ya know? Plus, with all the pressure, I think a McCaffrey on the ballot would help my dad."

His jaw dances with surprise. "You really think Janie Lee is an invisible sort of good?"

"Maybe she's not invisible . . . maybe we're just really loud?"

Woods gnaws on the collar of his shirt. He assesses. "No," he says. "Neither is true. And you really don't want to win a Corn Dolly?"

"And have every eye in town assessing me more than they already do? Have them voting if I am woman enough for the honor? Woods, even *you* put me on the guys' side of the Hexagon. I hardly think having attention on my femininity, or lack thereof, will help my dad keep his job. Plus, I would hate being paraded around town for scrutiny. Can you imagine what they would say?" I draw a banner with my right hand. "This candidate blew up a church. Vote for her."

He is quiet, respectful of my feelings. His shoulders are flat against the bed, his voice crawls upward like a vine on a trellis. "I hadn't thought of that." But in true Woods fashion, he fires another equally hard question. "How *are* things with your dad?"

Another round of silence.

"Don't be a badass with me, Elizabeth."

"I'm not."

He pins my shoulders, laughing. I squirm. He doesn't budge. "I'm your best friend, McCaffrey." *Well, there's a solid boundary,* I think. "If you believe us messing around on the roof excuses you from being real, you need a CAT scan. I've heard the rumors. I know there are people who want him gone, and I know what that means for you. Talk to me."

I execute a fairly sudden wrestling move that pins him under me. We're eyeball-to-eyeball—body-to-body. Intimate. "You're breaking the rules," I say.

"To call your shit your shit?"

I don't say anything.

"I've called your shit before," he reminds me. "And I plan to always do it. Every time I watch that gleam disappear from your eyes."

He has. Only once.

Puberty was reason number one Dad and I stopped being Dad and I. Reason number two was the Spandex Junkwagon Moms, a group of moms from church who push strollers and wear Lululemon when they aren't working out. One afternoon—I was thirteen, maybe fourteen—Woods was playing the piano in the sanctuary, and I was lying on a pew, listening, and tossing a football up to myself, when they appeared without warning. They took the football as a desecration of holy space and me as the son of Lucifer. They staged a coup, and after all the back-and-forthing, a small issue became a large issue in which I was at the center. Five families—five wealthy families—left our church, citing the reason as the unwilling-ness of Scott McCaffrey to discipline his sexually confused daughter. Principles, they claimed. Hypocrisy, they gossiped.

If I had a daughter like that I'd demand she wear girls' clothes.

If I had a daughter like that I'd send her to one of those camps.

If I had a daughter like that . . . they said.

My father had a daughter like that, and it became apparent to him, and later to me, that I wasn't the daughter he wished he had. Or maybe, I was the daughter he initially wanted—after all, he'd purchased the football and Nike gear—but in a battle of me versus the church, the church was the heavy-weight champion of the world. His job, our house, the family reputation: all meant I needed to stop playing football and start playing on Jesus's terms. (My father and Jesus being synony-mous entities.)

Which was the exact wrong thing to explain to Billie McCaffrey.

I decided that church members would never tell me what to do again. (Jesus could have his say—I was a person of faith; I just wasn't a person of legalistic bullshit.) Those women threw stones over a football and a girl who girled differently from them. That's the real problem—not people leaving the church, not Christians acting like Pharisees, not making up rules that don't exist.

Publicly, Dad held his ground about me. His daughter could wear what she wanted. His daughter wasn't disrespect-ing the sanctuary. His daughter was his daughter. Privately, my dad sided with them, and Mom sided with me.

I know. Because that's the moment he started trying to change me into someone else.

Mom's take on the situation was that those five families—she actually called the women "rich bitches"—didn't deserve to be part of our congregation, and they could mosey along. Dad's take was that Mom should dutifully bake and take a casserole to Margaret Lesley's house when she found out she had breast cancer. Mom made the casserole because of the cancer, but she made Dad deliver it to that Spandex Junkwagon because of me.

The one person who realized how much Dad's betrayal burrowed into my heart was Woods. I'd had a dad who I loved and respected. After that, I had a holy man who slept in a room down the hall.

Woods and I never made an arrangement about hiding these weaknesses. But we fell into a pattern. He's strong. I'm stronger. We're strongest. We act as if there are no failures, and we focus on the horizon. But I'd allowed him one true conversation about football and judgmental assholes, and he was now jonesing for another over my nongleaming brown eyes.

What would I say? There's no gleam because I'm scared we'll have to move or that even if we don't, I feel so close to misstepping, to losing everyone. Even him, my oldest and easiest friend. Please don't kiss me again. Please tell me what to do. Write me a plan on Einstein. Predetermine the course of my life.

Instead, I release my wrestling hold on Woods and say,

"You keep interrupting the best show on television, and I need you to stop."

We return to our side-by-side, temple-to-temple position. Woods isn't done. "You'd tell me if it was all too much, right? Because I swear to God, McCaffrey, if you're being a stoic bitch about this, and I find out later you're suicidal or using your saw to cut something other than two-by-fours, I'm gonna give you a real tombstone. You hear me?"

I nearly cave. I nearly open a vein and tell him everything. That I'm scared that if we fail at rescuing the Harvest Festival my dad will be ousted by the deacons and we'll have to move. And even if we don't have to move, I'll ruin this perfect thing—this Hexagon of people—because I don't understand what I want and need. I wish we could hook our brains together with an HDMI cable so he could just know, and I wouldn't have to say.

Janie Lee raises his window and crawls into the room and saves me.

"What's on the TV?" she calls.

Woods and I separate quickly, patting the space between us. Janie Lee vaults over Woods and lies down. She folds her hands over her stomach and there we are. Three peas in a pod, watching a television made of books.

"There's a variety show on," I suggest. "A cappella group."

They take the cue. The three of us are singing a mash-up of Adele and David Guetta when Woods's mom opens the door. "Morning, Billie. Janie Lee."

"Morning, Mrs. Carrington," Janie Lee and I say together.

She never seems surprised or fazed at two girls lying in the bed with her son, but today she's wearing an untraceable expression. Euphoria? No. Anticipation? Maybe. Hesitation? Yes.

From behind her back, she produces a newspaper. After popping her son in the forehead, she says, "I believe this is what you've been waiting for."

We sit up. I polish a little smudge on my boots—try to play this moment of anticipation cool. I hope to see *Mrs. Clare McCaffrey* in Times New Roman letters. Woods snatches the newspaper and reads the headline aloud: "Corn Dolly Results Announced."

He follows with three names:

Mrs. Tawny Jacobs

Mrs. Caroline Cheatham

Miss Elizabeth McCaffrey

If Janie Lee's mouth could catch a thousand flies, mine could catch a million.

Woods tugs his hat toward the bridge of his nose. "Hot damn, Elizabeth McCaffrey, you're on the ballot."

15

A man from Cambridge, of learned intelligence, published something called Littlewood's Law before I was born. The professor claimed mathematical proof that miracles occur once a month. Per person. Give or take. I don't know if this is science's doing or God's, but I am positive Billie McCaffrey on the Corn Dolly ballot is nothing short of miraculous. Last I checked, in the court of public opinion, I'd burned down a church.

With the unexpected news, my house has been downright festive. Mom fixes ribs, which is a banner that screams Special Occasion. Dad drinks a glass of champagne—an actual glass of alcohol—and invites the Hexagon and Grandy over to picnic. He's so stinking proud he'll have to pray for forgiveness all the way through the Harvest Festival.

I'm too stunned to be proud. Too concerned I might screw this up to enjoy anything more than their company.

Elizabeth McCaffrey, born 1999—d. ? R.I.P.: Corn Dolly Nominee.

By four thirty, paper plates are loaded with ribs and carbs. Napkins dance away from the picnic table at the wind's insistence. Mom plugs in festive white lights over the pergola even though the sun still hangs high above the tree line. When everyone sits, Dad lifts his glass. Aluminum beverages rise to shoulder height all around me. I duck my head and stare at my fork tines.

"To Billie," Dad says.

"To Billie," everyone repeats.

I am not the sort to cry, but I am nearly persuaded. Janie Lee, who is sitting directly across the table from me, puts an UGG on my boot, taps. Tears plop from her chin to her tank top and a quiet little "I'm proud of you" passes across the table like a scoop of mashed potatoes. At the other end, Woods winks and licks his lips. Possibly over the spicy rib seasonings. Possibly because he's spinning ideas into gold. *How do I turn a nomination into an award?* he's thinking.

Davey occupies the seat to my right; Mom, the one to my left. They have both wordlessly side-squeezed me. My dad seems taller than Molly the Corn Dolly. He stays tall through the whole meal, lavishing praise on everyone.

"You've all worked so hard," and "People were bound to notice," and "I'm proud of you." He doesn't hand these things to me alone; he speaks them to the whole Hexagon, and that makes me even happier.

When Mom says, "You're the first teenager ever to be nominated," I know she is trying to remind me that it might be a group accomplishment, but I need to own some of the excitement for myself.

I don't care if I win a Corn Dolly, but this, this full feeling in my soul, I'd like to keep it. Otters Holt is my home, and these people are my family.

One by one, they all tromp off to Saturday night plans. Grandy first: beauty sleep. Woods next: he's playing the piano for services tomorrow and hasn't practiced. Mash and Fifty follow, citing some Fantasy Football thing. Davey sticks around, making sure the trash is out, the lights are unplugged, and the propane tank is reattached to the grill.

"You working at the elementary school after church tomorrow?" he asks.

"If I don't die of shock in my sleep."

He leans in close. The stubble on his cheek grazes against my face. "You deserve this," he whispers, and then he is off and away; the Camaro has left the drive.

"You're very red," Janie Lee comments.

I've been red-faced since I saw the newspaper.

"Let's go somewhere," she says.

We tumbleweed to our bikes and pedal furiously down the drive without so much as an explanation to Mom and Dad. River Run Road is short and pockmarked. We weave back and forth, avoiding as many potholes as we can. Sometimes our hands are on the bars, sometimes high in the air; we take back road to back road, which eventually spits us out near Molly the Corn Dolly and the dam overlook. I am windblown and spectacularly happy. The light bends golden and glowing over the horizon and trees. Perhaps I've been alive seventeen years. Perhaps three hundred. On a day like today, age is irrelevant: existence is infinite.

The leaves aren't afire yet, but the orange and red and yellow of autumn are on preorder. One more rain and Otters Holt will start to explode with colors. Molly the Corn Dolly greets us. A family, using a tripod, snaps a quick photo before piling back into a Suburban.

Janie Lee points toward the overlook. "The dam?"

I pedal in that direction, and once we arrive I toss my bike in the grass, walking directly up to the concrete barrier. I bend over to see the water. The deep blue and frothing lake is a mirror for the sky, but it is not transparent. Visibility stops within inches of the surface. Beautiful things are often muddy.

Janie Lee is beside me. "There," she says of a barge carrying coal or maybe limestone.

I nod, hoping the light will hold long enough for us to watch it go through the lock.

A towboat chugs forward, pushes the barge to the left, nearly to the shore. Even from this height, the cacophony of water and machinery keeps us from speaking. When the barge is in place, the towboat backs downriver and the massive lock doors inch closed. Turbines grind and water slips out of tiny holes, starting the laborious process of changing the water level inside the lock. All because someone effing brilliant imagined a seventy-five-foot elevator for boats.

Concrete and steel.

Water sucking, snorting, draining, or filling.

Magical engineering at its very best.

I feel a strange kinship with this incredible but very normal feat. Isn't it as unlikely as I am? Isn't it magic the same way me being nominated is magic? I say as much to Janie Lee.

"Billie," Janie Lee protests.

"Shhhhh." The water levels are almost flush with the other side of the Tennessee, the enchantment almost at an end.

"Don't ruin today with your doubts," she tells me.

They aren't doubts. They're questions. Why the sudden shift in town opinion? How did someone who has been called dykish so often she practically answers to it make it onto the ballot? The Corn Dolly is not a beauty contest, but raw beauty is always a consideration. Gerry called me beautiful. I am trying to think who I would call beautiful. My mom. Jeanelle. Mrs. Carrington. They are polished and pearled and feminine.

Janie Lee. Those long legs covered by skinny jeans that get lost in her UGGs. That black sweatshirt of mine she grabbed from the garage, the front hoodie pocket slight torn. It matches her hair. Matches the heavy mascara highlighting her eyes. Yes, she's beautiful. Maybe even striking.

But I am the girl-who-isn't-a-guy who lives perpetually on

the guys' side. A brother, a dude, a . . .

I climb onto the concrete barrier as though it is the chest freezer in my garage and swing my legs. Janie Lee follows. It is now almost too dark to see anything more than the shadowy outlines of the other side of the lake. We've lost complete sight of the barge. But we let ourselves be absorbed by nature around us. Chirping crickets and scrambling squirrels. They are harmonizing in a nearby stand of trees. A barred owl sings the song of a whinnying horse. Somewhere below us, a fisherman revs a boat engine and heads home to clean his catch.

"Can you believe it?" I ask.

"I can. You've done a lot of things to put yourself in that position, friend." She reels off a list that is basically one item: helping old people.

"It doesn't seem like enough."

"Don't be silly. Just enjoy it. Your mom is happy. Your dad is positively enraptured. I swear, B, it's like he just got to baptize the whole town. Accept the fact that people see the real you."

The real me is a cloudy, fuzzy thing these days.

"Are you excited? Even a little?" she asks.

"I'm . . . overwhelmed."

"And delighted?"

"It still feels like a fluke, you know? Maybe we shouldn't talk about it."

She swings sideways. Puts her feet up on my thighs and shoves her hands in the hoodie pocket. "You know what we should talk about?" A pause. "Woods."

"O-kay." I keep swinging my legs, pounding my heels against the concrete.

"I was wrong," she says. "The night of the fire."

"Oh."

"Tuesday night, after practice, he kissed me. Or I kissed him. Either way, we kissed. We had finished singing. I was packing away my violin, and he was shoving sheet music into his backpack and he just came out with it. 'We should kiss. Billie said we should kiss. And I'd like to so I can stop thinking about it.' Can you believe that? Well, I guess you can if you told him to do it, or maybe he's already told you this story."

"He hasn't."

"And so we had an awkward moment where we worked out if it was okay with me. Which of course it was. You know I'd been thinking about it too. Except we were both worried that if it stank, our musical partnership might change. It's funny the things you think about when you should just be feeling, isn't it?"

"Yeah." I desperately want her to get to the heart of it. Tuesday night was five days ago. Five full days of seeing them nearly all day, and I picked up on nothing. Nada. They hadn't even sat near each other tonight.

"So, the kiss, yeah, nope."

"Huh," I say. *So, the kiss, yeah, nope*: exactly how I felt. "Did you talk about it?"

"Yeah. I said, 'That was sort of like dropping a book on the lower register of a piano.' And he said, 'Whelp, that's that,' and *dusted his hands.* Billie, he dusted his hands. That's how bad it was."

"Did he bite your lip or something?" I ask.

"No. He's decent enough at kissing. It was because"—the palm of her hand lays flat on my stomach, above my belly button—"I don't love Woods from here, from my gut. I love him from my head, from our history. I just got confused."

I knew the feeling well. "It's easy to get confused when you've got great people in your life."

"Right? Don't tell him I said this, but honestly, I had more going in the guts region when I kissed Mash."

I whip around. "You've kissed Mash?"

She scrunches and takes her hand off my stomach. "You haven't?"

"I kissed Fifty once."

Her turn to scrunch and push me. "You kissed Fifty? When? Why do we even have that silly code if everyone has kissed everyone?"

"Everyone has not kissed everyone," I say, locking eyes on a dock across the lake whose decorative pink lights have started flashing.

"Nearly everyone." She moves closer, and returns to the posture she assumed when we first arrived. Feet hanging over the side, body slouched, hands back in the hoodie pocket. "You should kiss Davey. He's into you."

"I probably will if he's not into Thomas," I say, because maybe I'd like that. He has very nice lips, and he's easy to talk to.

Should I tell her I also kissed Woods? I could, but it doesn't matter now.

"To be honest," she tells me, "I'm a little bit relieved. About Woods, I mean. It takes a lot of energy to like someone. And since Tuesday . . . I've felt better, lighter. It wouldn't have worked anyway. Not only is he going to die in the 42045 zip code, someone will probably construct a forty-foot statue of Woods Carrington right next to Molly."

"I'm glad you feel easier about things."

"Me too."

"Just friends is easier," she says.

"Just friends is easier," I repeat.

She leans her head against my shoulder, and we wait to pedal home until there are uncountable stars.

16

B illie, stop rocking on two legs. You'll break the chair."
Mom beckons my brain back to the dinner table and looks
past me to the television.

The New Madrid Fault Line rang like a rotary phone for
four or five seconds yesterday—only a 3.5—and the newscasters
are acting like we've never had an earthquake before. It happened during church and was over so fast no one even thought
to get under the pews. It also happened while the church was
recognizing—by standing ovation—that the preacher's daughter had been nominated for the Corn Dolly.

"You don't think the two things are connected?" a lady
asked another in a way that suggested she most certainly
thought they were.

"The Lord works in mysterious ways," one gentleman replied.

I wish Dad hadn't overheard that.

He hasn't brought it up, because he's focused on a more earth-shaking conversation he had with Davey's mom at the BI-LO, which is not technically BI-LO anymore, but we can't be bothered to call it Greg's Market.

"Clare!" He often addresses my mother as though I am not at the table. "I ran into Hattie Winters today at BI-LO, and she looks like she could use someone to talk to. I wondered if you might phone her up or invite her to coffee."

A typical pastor's wife job. He traffics in souls; it's her job to traffic in hearts. I am currently trafficking in roast beef, mashed potatoes drowning in gravy, and three bags of LEGOs on my placemat. The LEGOs have priority. I try to bring a distraction to the table that isn't my life.

Dad, wanting my mother to pay attention to him instead of the news, says her name as if she is deaf. When that doesn't work, he taps the tines against her plate. "Clare, did you hear me?"

"They're showing coverage of the quake," she explains. The news channel shows a picture of the elementary school, looking far better than it did two weeks ago, but several windows are broken.

I was on that roof recently, I think. *I was on that roof falling out of love with Woods.*

We have a small television in our kitchen that has one channel when Dad's around: Fox News. It is this nine-inch screen that my parents squint at now rather than the fifty-five inches of HD beauty in the living room, also visible from the kitchen table. My mother wipes her mouth with a napkin. Folds the cloth into a triangle and places it neatly in her lap. She gives my father her full attention.

He says, "I wish someone would buy the school and tear it down. It's an eyesore."

I sit bolt upright. Four chair legs on the floor.

He continues, "Nothing useful will ever happen there again."

So many useful things have already happened there. Who would have thought that a game of Beggar and a kiss could change the future? That school is directly responsible for my surname never being Carrington. I hope it will soon be responsible for saving the Harvest Festival.

Mom gently guides the discussion back to where it was previously going. "What were you saying about Hattie, Scott?"

He crams another bite into his mouth. "She could use someone to talk to."

I'm adding LEGO bricks to my prototype of the elementary school, the very one my father wants to tear down, but I'm listening intently.

Dad speaks again. "You know everything she's been through. First, John. Then losing her dad. And now . . . Davey."

If we were a normal family, my mom would give my dad *a look*, and they would finish this discussion far from my ears. I've seen the Carringtons employ this tactic.

"What's wrong with Davey?" Mom asks.

Dad checks in—I am a blank page—and answers, "Hattie was hinting that he might be gay. That maybe he'd experimented with a friend in Nashville, and he's . . . I don't know, dating someone? Billie, what do you know about that? I mean, I've noticed the eyeliner. But when I was your age I loved grunge bands and they used plenty of eyeliner and seemed pretty hetero. So I didn't assume. Maybe Hattie is assuming."

"Maybe she is." Mom shrugs. "Maybe she's not."

Dad ignores Mom and taps his fork near my LEGOs. "I'm asking you."

Lumpy mashed potatoes have never tasted so good. I fill my mouth, lift my shoulders as if I give zero shits.

This doesn't suit him. "Come on, you have to know something. She needs some comfort."

"Dad," I say, using universal eye contact for *I'm not answering that.*

His head whips toward Mom. "Clare?"

A simple tone that has come to mean: *control your offspring.*

Being nominated for the Corn Dolly clearly doesn't fix everything.

"Elizabeth"—Mom is typically the only person who calls me Elizabeth, and she only does so when she's caught between

Dad and me—"he's not asking you to betray your friend's confidence. He's asking if Hattie has any reason to be concerned. Right, Scott?"

"No," Dad asserts. "I'm asking if Davey Winters is sexually fluid."

Despite my best efforts, my tongue nearly licks the carpet. Sexually fluid? When did Dad zoom out of his century and into mine? Some preachers' conference over the last year? "Dad, we don't . . . we don't talk about sexuality."

"Please! I've read books about this. I've listened to podcasts and they all say your generation doesn't care to define sexuality," he says with all the confidence of an expert.

I curl tighter into my chair.

"There's a whole alphabet of letters. L-G-B-T-Q-I-A-B-C-D—"

"Dad."

"Oh, Scott, you've embarrassed her," Mom says.

Dad slaughters roast beef with a steak knife, lifts his fork, and chews a tine long after the meat is gone. "Hattie is the one who seemed embarrassed. She's troubled over this, feels like her son's not talking to her."

I'm instantly pissed off on Davey's behalf. Why would he talk to his mother about his sexuality if she seemed even slightly embarrassed? Before I remember I'm talking to Brother Scott McCaffrey, I say, "Would it be so bad if Davey were gay?"

"See?" Dad says to Mom. "I told you, they *have* talked about it."

"No, we haven't," I say.

His retort is a classic parental redirect. "Please take the LEGOs off the table."

"This has nothing to do with LEGOs." I've built far more unusual things at this table while they talked to each other. If the diorama of my favorite Marvel scene made entirely of colored toothpicks didn't piss him off, LEGOs certainly shouldn't. I shove my plate off the placemat. The fork rattles on the plate. The knife falls to the floor.

He huffs. "I don't understand what I've done to make you so unhappy. Clare, we've raised the most difficult child on the planet."

"Scott! That's ridiculously untrue."

"*Clare.*"

My parents love each other, but neither of them loves the way the other deals with me.

"I'm full." I'm up and in the kitchen using scalding-hot water to rinse my plate before Mom can say, "Billie, you don't have to leave."

I sweep LEGOs into a bowl I swipe from the counter and walk to the garage with Dad yelling at the back of my head. "Why am I the bad guy for caring about Hattie?"

"Why am I the bad guy for caring about Davey?"

"I should ground you from the gar—"

I slam the door.

Less than twenty-four hours ago, my father raised a glass on my behalf. That is the potential of us. The reality of us is me dumping LEGOs on a workbench, finishing my replica, and setting the display on a belt sander. I take out my cell phone, turn on the sander, and record an earthquake. I'm judging it to be 5.2 on the LEGO Richter scale while the argument coming from inside my house is an 8.

The LEGOs explode all over the floor.

I am nostalgic for a time when my family slathered butter on popcorn and watched *Survivor* reruns on the living room couch. I am nostalgic for parents I don't have. What would it be like to be raised by a couple who say things like "Fall in love with a person, Billie," rather than a minister who says things like "Hate the sin and love the sinner"? I am smart enough to understand that Dad's conversation with Hattie was also about me. There among the subtext, he's asking a question.

I wait for the yelling to stop before I slink to my room and fall into bed fully clothed.

That night, I dream I am a guy. One hundred percent all-American boy.

There's no easing into the dream. No sense of being asleep. I close my eyes, and when my brain wakes up, I have a penis and a problem.

I live in the same saltbox parsonage. My father is still an issue. My mother is made of monograms and flowy shirts. My Grandy is still a thunder cat. I have the same friends. Own the same clothes. But I ride a green bike to school. My real bike is black.

Woods calls me dude and bro and hits me on the shoulder.

Mash throws up. Fifty makes sex jokes. Davey is missing.

These things are banked in my dream memory, and I am aware of being me as I move through the dream. Only . . . Dream Me is a dude.

I am in the youth room. There is a wine cooler on the floor and an unopened bag of Twizzlers peeks out from behind the couch cushion. There is a stack of Bibles there too. I think . . . I am going to hell for this. Einstein says WAYS FOR BILLY TO EMBARRASS SCOTT.

I am on the couch with Janie Lee.

She's wearing her big, gaudy glasses, and she is under me. Entwined with me. Her UGGs are scattered, as if she took them off in a hurry. The soft flannel of her pajamas is against my leg hair. I slide my hand under the black Victoria's Secret cami she wears beneath her sweatshirt and tug until it's over her head. The sweatshirt that is already on the floor. The sweatshirt I pulled off her.

I inch my fingers around to her spine and press my chest against hers. She is insanely warm, but shivering.

I am shirtless. She's kissing my Adam's apple; working her mouth around my neck, under my chin. I didn't shave today, and the way she's kissing me tickles. I am familiar with this body I've had for dream seconds, as if I've had it for years.

"Shhhhh," she tells me. "We're going to wake up Mash and Fifty."

She says *shhhhh*, but doesn't say *stop*. She means, *Be quieter, Billie. Don't let them catch us.* They are propped on the opposite couch five feet away. Mash is wearing one of those Breathe Right strips over his nose. Fifty's snoring. Even though it's blazing hot, I stretch a fuzzy blanket over us in case they wake up. We whisper. We giggle. I want to know every part of her.

I am scared of being caught. But I am terrified of losing her or hurting her or going too quickly. I want to live on this couch for the rest of my life.

Neither of us is scared this is the wrong thing. She is worth polishing all the pews in every church in America if we are caught. Worth all the service projects we might be assigned. Worth my father hating me.

I tell her that.

She touches my stomach like she did the night at the dam and says, "I feel love right here."

"Me too."

Mash coughs once, twice, three times. Smoke seeps under the door, starts rolling in like a fog. It is somehow dark in the room and light enough to see gray clouds consuming the mini fridge. Consuming Einstein. The church alarms go off, the phone rings, and I think, *Please don't interrupt us. Why didn't we put a Do Not Disturb sign on Youth Suite 201?*

"Mash cooked socks in the microwave again," she says.

"Yeah," I say, as if I care about Mash right now.

Around the room, there is suddenly an orchestra—every player a twin of Janie Lee. Violins, cellos, upright bass, viola. With perfect timing the musicians draw fingers and bows across the strings, manipulating the air with an emotional, haunting melody.

Janie Lee tastes like Gerry. She tastes like music. We're biting each other's lips. I lean away from her, realizing again how beautiful she is.

The orchestra sounds like it's grieving.

How I love her glasses. Her toothpaste has Scope in it. Her blush smells like sandalwood. The song is between us. I taste her soul on my tongue.

I promise I won't tell Woods that this happened.

She says, "No one has to know."

Gray clouds of smoke engulf Mash and Fifty. The cello is the only instrument I hear.

Dad bangs on the door. "Billie, the church is on fire. Billie."

"Ignore him," I say.

"Ignore everyone."

"I love you."

Words I've never said in real life.

"I love you too."

We keep right on kissing until the flames singe our skin.

17

Six hours have passed since I put my head on my pillow. Five minutes have passed since I woke up from that dream. *That* dream. *That* sex dream.

My first sex dream. My first sex anything.

And . . . I was a guy.

And . . . I was with Janie Lee.

And . . . I don't know what to think about anything.

Light spills into my room through my curtains. Mom's frying bacon in the kitchen. I don't have any clean socks. Morning is here. Morning doesn't care about my sexuality.

Jesus, when I see Janie Lee in first period, I'll be thinking about that thing she did with her tongue instead of dangling participles. That's an improvement to language arts, but a danger to friendship.

Before I further question my sexuality, I consult the internet's opinion on sex dreams. According to "experts" I am starved for intimacy and have "a masculine mind-set." "No," I tell the internet, and then scroll mindlessly through Janie Lee's Instagram account, registering photos of her, the Hexagon, and us. In each one, her expression is unshakable. Even when we're all making silly faces, there she is, perfect mascara and straight white teeth.

There's one particular photo from three months ago. It was taken at the wedding chapel on Highway 62. Woods and Janie Lee share a piano bench. Violin in her lap, grin on her face: she's full, bright. Woods has his mouth open, singing. His hair is gelled as straight as it'll go; he looks about ninety-five years old. The caption reads *Carson Wedding #fallingslowly #once #happyforthem #happyforme*.

Janie Lee's wearing a sexy black dress. And I suppose it strikes me for the first time that dress clothes are like jewelry—accessories to skin. I've been using wardrobe as a fuck-you statement for so long that it hasn't occurred to me clothes aren't what I'm seeing when I look at Janie Lee. It's her in all her Janie Lee–ness. The same way I put on different clothes and went to a costume party with Davey, I can costume any part of myself I want.

Twenty minutes later, I'm in the kitchen sporting one of my two funeral dresses. A juice glass smashes against the porcelain tile. Shards and slivers land in the grout. Glass scatters all the way to the laundry room.

"Did you . . . lose a bet?" Mom asks, but not cruelly. "Or is it one of those specialty dress-up days?"

I might not get fancy very often, but I understand the requirements. Real bra. Grandy's necklace. Mascara and lip gloss. By God, I am even wearing a thong. These are items I own because my mother has to buy me something for Christmas each year that is not LEGOs and odd art supplies.

I'm uncomfortable as hell, and as hot as I can manage.

"Yes, of course I did, because that's the only way I am capable of dressing up." This sarcasm is superior to explaining that my best friends mistook me for a dude and, double whammy, I had a sex dream where I was the guy.

When she refuses my help with the glass, I pour orange juice and await additional commentary. Mom's staring over her bifocals, directly at my breasts; I wish she didn't appear so stupefied. "You do look incredible, Billie."

When someone dies, I safety pin the neckline. Without the pin, I have the illusion of cleavage. "I'm a frickin' clown," I say.

"Don't say frickin', baby. It means the same thing as that other word."

Dad arrives in the kitchen waving the morning newspaper. "Clare, did you see this? Tawny Jacobs is on the front page." Last night's argument is gone. He hasn't noticed Mom sweeping glass into a plastic bag. He keeps babbling about the festival without having her attention—he has a gift for this. "This article is basically rubbish. Ada May's supposed to be impartial, but I swear she's advocating for—"

He sees me. If he had a glass, it would also be broken. He tosses the newspaper on the table and presses a kiss against my cheek. I am pinned against his suit coat, against the front pocket where he always carries a tiny Moleskine notebook and fountain pen.

"Did someone die?" he asks.

"No one died. I did not lose a bet. I wanted to wear a dress."

Dad kisses my cheek again. He does not know Littlewood's Law by name, but his expression titles this a miracle. "This getup is perfect timing."

Mom dumps the dustpan of glass in the trash. From the clanking and slamming, she doesn't like the implications of "perfect timing." We concern ourselves momentarily with breakfast. Toast, coffee, bacon. I've missed the Hexagon at the elementary school to do this, and have to text Woods for a pickup. I'm pressing Send and then removing crumbs from my bodice when Mom prompts Dad to explain why it's *perfect* timing.

He taps the newspaper article with the photo of Tawny. "We're all going to need to be on our best behavior with the Corn Dolly stuff."

I shouldn't ask. I do anyway. "What about me wearing a dress puts us on 'our best behavior'?"

You know, his slack jaw says.

"I gotta go," I tell them before I start another fight Mom has to finish. Yeah, Dad, me wearing a dress is like a receiving a Crown of Righteousness from God himself.

"Take a coat," he yells. "Chilly out today."

I clomp to the front deck and await Woods's pickup. The day is every shade of blue and one or two shades of gray. Warm air comes from the west, cool from the east. It'll storm before lunch. Woods'll probably have his own commentary on my attire. He might even think I'm trying to impress him, which I hadn't considered when I got dressed. No matter what he says, I will girl to the fullest girl today.

Eight hours later, I wish I'd worn a steel corset.

Here are stats on a day with Billie in a dress:

41: Classmates who reference the apocalypse upon sight of me.

1: who questions if I triggered the earthquake.

53: Double takes I witness. (A lowball estimate; I couldn't possibly have seen them all.)

17: Catcalls.

9: Times Fifty says, "Damn, McCaffrey."

2: Times Mash offers to get an umbrella so I won't get rained on while going to the C wing. "You sure, B? It's no big deal," he promises, even though he has never offered me an umbrella before.

4: Comments from the girls who often hassle me. They say, "OMG, Dyke Bike, someone should have nominated you years ago."

I've been Dyke Bike to them since seventh grade. In fairness, I called them things too. But I've managed to go years without mentioning that their cumulative IQ is a number I can count on one hand.

I tolerate everything for the sake of two compliments. When I scooted into Woods's truck this morning, he said, "That's a 9.2 on the Richter, Elizabeth McCaffrey," and Janie Lee followed his comment with, "No, it's a 10." Neither of them asked me why. Maybe they still felt guilty about Einstein.

The person who asks why is Davey.

The last bells rings. I'm careening toward the parking lot with the rest of OHHS, eyes on the books in my arms. A body, tall and compact, falls into purposeful step with my boots. "You're coming with me," Davey says. The Camaro transports us to my house first. I am told to return to the car in comfortable clothes because we're going on an adventure. Under this circumstance, I do not mind being told what to do.

I shed the dress and thong, leaving clothing strewn across my bedroom. When I settle into Davey's front seat wearing black athletic pants and a T-shirt, the pent-up parts of me finally free, I flap my knees about widely as if I have been wearing a straitjacket.

"Where are we going?" I ask.

"Somewhere I love."

"Why?" I say instead of asking where.

"Why the runway event?" he answers. This is a brand-new

question, not just a repeat of mine. He wants an explanation for the dress.

Ignore him, be sarcastic, tell the truth? I weigh the options equally and say, "I'm still working that out. I needed to know if I could."

"Because of the Hexagon of Love? Or the Corn Dolly?"

"Well, *that* happened," I say.

"Not many things unnerve you, Billie McCaffrey, but that board did," he says sympathetically. "Well . . . not many things unnerve you in a way you can't hide."

I draw my legs under me, cross my arms over my chest. "Give me your theory."

"O-kay," he starts. "Thinking of yourself as boyish is one thing, but your friends assigned you a gender—without asking—and that flayed you. If I had to speculate, you're actually upset because you believe they should know you well enough to avoid such an error. Which isn't totally fair to you or them. Gender, sexuality, fluidity: those areas require stumbling around in the dark, feeling, and bumping into things. But even if you can admit that, you still feel out of control. And probably lonely." No stutter. No question. He delivers this analysis as if he has thought about it all day long.

I find my fist unwittingly clenched around the door handle. Except I am not angry with him. This experiment: why did I do it? Janie Lee's Instagram account? Proving Woods and Einstein wrong? I hate dresses.

"Please don't be mad. You asked for the theory," he says

quietly, eyes never leaving the road.

I retaliate with a single sentence. "Why did you put Elizabeth Rawlings on the board when we both know she's not your first choice?"

"Woods put Elizabeth Rawlings on the board," he answers.

Davey is inside himself thinking inside thoughts. I'm inside myself hating how exposed I feel. He interrupts with another conclusion. "You give him too much power."

Woods has always been serenely controlling. I've always gone along, easy breezy, because in elementary school I didn't have the skill to make deep connections on my own. Woods made them all for me. Tied up friends with neat little bows and presented them to me like birthday presents. "For you, Billie McCaffrey," he seemed to say of Fifty and Mash and himself. He saw I was oddly confident and confidently odd, which meant I was wildly unpopular. And lonely.

Part of me gets lonely landing on these pre-Woods memories.

I am the one who acquired Janie Lee and welcomed her to the group, but Woods is the one who cemented her feet in place.

I took for granted that they knew me. I took for granted that Woods would always be right.

There's another truth here. One I'd rather not look at dead on. Maybe, when it comes to sexuality, my foregone conclusions are not all that foregone. Sometimes tomboys are gay. Sometimes they're not. I wonder which kind of tomboy I am or if there is room to not know until later.

"Tell me," he says softly.

"I . . ." When I left my room this morning, I thought I'd never admit the sex dream to anyone. Not ten hours later, I want to ladle these thoughts from my head into Davey's soup bowl. "Have you ever had a dream about someone?" I ask.

"Sure."

"Like a dream-dream? A *dream*."

"Billie, everyone has dream-dreams."

"Not like this," I say.

He asks for the details. I hit the high points quick and fast—guy, sex, Janie Lee. He shifts in his seat, considers a response. "I'm glad you're not carrying this around by your-self," he says first. "I don't think it necessarily means you're gay or transgender. And no one is asking you to choose because of a whiteboard or a sex dream."

"I know."

"But you still feel pressured to choose?"

"I feel pressured to assess," I say. "It all has to mean some-thing. But I can't tell if my being attracted to Janie Lee means I'm attracted to girls."

"So, do you think there's any chance that's how she feels about you?"

"Maybe."

"And do you think you're not overly excited about the Corn Dolly because you're wrestling with what it means to be a girl?"

"Maybe."

He says, "I think that's normal."

"I feel stupid that I didn't see this coming. I've always been so fixated on a future with Woods, and she was right there too. I should have realized."

"Why?"

"Because I should have."

"We all have blind spots, Billie."

I release my grip on the door handle. "I don't want things to change, *and* I want the freedom to explore. Am I even making sense?"

"You *are* making sense." He reaches for the tie hanging from the rearview mirror, stops, grips the wheel instead. "What does your gut say?"

"My gut . . . well, my gut put on a dress this morning thinking it was a solution, so let's not go with my gut right now."

"Let's take this stuff one decision at a time. Are you sure you're over Woods? I have a hard time believing you've been in love with him forever and now, poof, all gone, game over. On to Janie Lee."

"It's not poof, all gone. More like a switch flipped. More like I wasn't actually in love to begin with. We kissed . . ."

"And . . ."

The passing cornfields are devoid of color, the gray sky swallowing their radiance. I tell him everything. It comes out of me fast—liquid being sucked from a two-liter bottle.

Gulping. Fizzy. Gone. "So there's nothing sexual between us. Like literally nothing," I conclude.

"Oh."

"Is it wrong that I want more than that?" I'm asking as if he is an expert, when really I have no idea.

"You should be with someone who makes you the best version of yourself," he says.

"Like you are with Thom?" I ask, gently probing.

He averts his eyes from the road. "What makes you say that?"

"Well, when you're with him, your face relaxes."

"Hmmm."

Hmmm, I love him? Hmmm, he makes me feel safe? Hmmm, I don't know about Thom any more than you know about Janie Lee?

At this cue, he commandeers the radio and forces me to listen to Lyle Lovett and David Bowie. I am tired from my confessions. As I'm nodding off, he strokes the tie hanging from his rearview mirror with longing and I wonder if he misses his father.

When he nudges me awake, we're parked in a driveway.

"Where are we?" I ask.

"Not somewhere my face relaxes. Not yet," he replies.

18

Large white columns stretch two stories to meet an impressive rectangular roof. The house belongs on the coast. With its large porches, stacked one on top of the other, an American flag hanging from the topmost railing. With its off-white siding, black shutters, and heavily manicured landscaping that perfectly frames every corner and edge with a splash of color. It is not that the house itself couldn't exist in Otters Holt—we do have some hundred-year-old architecture. But there would be toys in the yard, or perhaps a large ornamental chicken, or maybe algae on the siding, or even a *Beware of Dog* sign tacked to the tree in the front. It would be lived-in. This house was built like a display—not to play with or abide in, but simply to exist.

"This is where I grew up," he says. It doesn't take a genius to see he is embarrassed. "We're going to meet Gerry and Thom later for dinner, but I need to pick something up first."

When he opens the car door to get out, I do the same.

It is nearly five o'clock. I ask, "Will your dad be home?"

"I hope not. I'll text him later and say I stopped by to get a few things from downstairs."

I stay close, just behind, choosing not to walk in step with him. He unlocks the front door and walks so swiftly through the entry hall that I don't have time to think anything except: the inside aesthetic matches the outside. Davey opens one of several doors in a side hallway. Steps lead down. We take them two at a time, arriving in a large open space that is outfitted the way Youth Suite 201 should be: pool table, five arcade games, a working foosball table.

I do not tell him this room is nice. He knows.

He's acting cagey, and I have to guess what he's thinking. I halfway regret getting out of the car and intruding in this space while simultaneously feeling better that he does not have to be here alone.

He rummages in a closet, and I stay behind, bouncing a pool ball along the rails with my hand, hoping this will end soon.

"You need anything?" I call.

"No, but come see this if you want."

We've created many memories since he moved to Otters Holt, but my picture of him is still full of holes. I like being invited to fill in the spaces.

He's squatting on the floor, searching for something. We are inside an oversize closet that is more organized than my garage has ever dreamed of being, and equally interesting. Large wire racks line the left and right walls. Bins are labeled: *eye makeup, clown, horror, Marvel, jewelry black, jewelry gold, jewelry colorful*. There must be a hundred plastic storage boxes—some very large, containing toy guns and swords, and some very small, promising colored hair and skin. One long closet bar hangs across the back of the closet. Costumes are wedged between the walls.

"This is all yours?" I ask.

"Mine and Dad's."

My assumptions about John Winters did not include someone who played dress-up. It turns out Davey is not rummaging around after all. He's working from a specific list, searching from bin to bin, taking required items and filling a duffel at his feet. I do not interrupt again, imagining all the people he has been in this room: Captain America, d'Artagnan, a banana— that's the only thing the costume in the far corner could be.

He sees my expression of wonder and misreads it as judgment. "I'm a dork," he says.

"This, my friend, is something far beyond dork." Before I can add, *It's amazing*, he flashes a hurt expression. "I mean, I knew you were into this from the costume party, but I didn't know you had an actual Bat Cave."

"Dad calls it my Bunker of Personalities."

"I see why."

"Did he do this with you?"

He scowls and grabs an item. "The only costume Dad wears is skin. He pretends to be human. The only reason he tolerates this obsession is because I'm good at it."

"When you say good at it, what do you mean?"

"Well, I've won the LaserCon contest the last five years."

I spend a long minute examining Bat Cave Davey, realizing he has not only given up Thom to be in Otters Holt with his mom, he has given up other precious things. This is his garage. And it explains why he's decent at eyeliner when I still cannot manage a straight line.

"Gerry said LaserCon is coming up."

"Yeah. I don't have any chance of winning this year, but I can't show up naked."

He's painting a picture of himself. A champion who doesn't have to win to enjoy something. I admire this. And simultaneously know that John Winters would not admire anything about this sentiment. I've only met him once, but his thorns were showing.

Davey shoulders the bag, flips the light off, and says, "I was thinking about you in that dress today. It felt like my closet. Like a costume rather than an outfit. It might showcase a piece of you, but not all of you."

My tongue presses against the back of my teeth in thought. Yes, he is right.

We are up the steps and in the kitchen sneaking bottled water when we hear the back door open, the security system dinging that John Winters is home. He strides into the kitchen, trapping us. Davey has his long face and high cheekbones and forehead. His dad has worn khakis, button-downs, and sweater vests for so long that if he died, the clothes would go to work the next day without him. His keys rattle in a catch-all ceramic bowl. His voice does not rattle. "I told you," he begins.

"I know," Davey says.

What he has told him is unclear. Not to come here? Not to bring anyone over? I want to slip out the front door, but I don't leave. John Winters is the kind of man who makes you straighten your back. I straighten my back and pretend I am welcome.

"You're the *pallbearer*," he says at me rather than to me.

I'll admit, the smear is so judgmental; my shoulders fall a centimeter or two.

"We're leaving, Dad," Davey says.

For a moment, I believe John Winters will cave. His face, well, it looks like it wants to say things his pride will not allow. I do not doubt he loves Davey. I do doubt he has ever shown that to his son. And as if to prove my theory correct, he says, "If you want your stuff, you have to come home. I told you that when you left with Mom."

Davey is still except for his fingers. They flex, knuckles white and knobby, around the straps of the duffel. I am still as well, trying hard to avoid blinking so I won't miss a single nuance. While I am watching his hands, Davey drops the bag on the granite floor. Drops. Not flings. Not slams. Just a single uncurling that says he is letting go of something far more important than the contents of the duffel.

He fights so quietly.

We leave.

Music in the Camaro cranks loudly from the speakers when he turns the engine. We reach the power knob at the same time, our index fingers on top of each other's, and I say, "I'll build you a costume. Any costume you want," and he says, "Thank you," but we don't look at each other. So I don't know if he's crying, but I am.

I want what any child wants: for my father to be proud of me. For Dad to look into me, and say, "You are good," rather than to look at me and say, "You are not good enough."

The Corn Dolly decision, my wavering feelings on Janie Lee: I will either play the game and miss finding out the truth—or I will explore the truth and lose the game. Only it's not a game. Because games go back in boxes and get stacked away with other games. This nomination, this competition, has real stakes.

I know the cost. It's the same price Davey paid just four months ago: a town, a house, a parent, a move, a hobby, friends.

19

W e while away thirty minutes, driving through parks and subdivisions and trafficked streets. He shows me Waylan Academy. Its warm redbrick walls and avenue of Bradford pear trees leading from one section of campus to another, ending at a sports complex that's worth millions and millions of donations. It looks like a small college campus, which is about what I'd worked out in my head before the tour.

Text messages are pinging his phone every few seconds; Gerry and Thom are starving, Gerry is finally off work, Thom is picking her up. They'll meet us in five minutes at Pizza Pans, because, as Gerry puts it, "My stomach is snacking on my small intestine."

I have my own set of messages. Mom's *Will you be home for supper? Nope.* Dad's *I thought y'all were community servicing after school*, even though he knows Janie Lee and Woods practice on Tuesday evenings and it's the one night we took off. *Nope.* There are messages from Janie Lee and Woods. Practice night usually means, *We're on Mars, leave a message*, but me wearing a polyester blend dress was either a sign of my declining emotional state or a massive victory.

Janie Lee: *You looked amazing today.*

Me: *Thanks.*

Janie Lee: *Don't take this the wrong way.*

Me: *I won't.*

Janie Lee: *I think I still like you better in jeans.*

Me: *Good.*

The dream comes storming into my thoughts. We're fine, I tell myself. She said it the other night: Just friends is better. But I still stop a moment and pray. I haven't prayed much since that morning of watercolor light on Mash's floor; the morning after Big T died and it felt like God himself was spilling into the room, just so we wouldn't have to be alone in our grief. There are people who do not pray, and I understand why. It's a strange thing to talk to someone you can't see if you've never tried it. But for me it's really a very nice and safe feeling. Like putting your toes in warm sand at the beach or stepping into the shower after a long day.

But here, in the recesses of my heart, I am honest. Three words I repeat without speaking:

I am afraid. I am afraid. I am afraid. I am afraid. God, I am very afraid.

This is my deepest well, and I have dropped a coin to the very bottom.

We leave Waylan for the restaurant. We are parked, and I am wrung out.

On our trip across the parking lot, Thom hugs everyone. He's inclusive, always drawing people closer. He musses my hair and tells Davey, "This is the face of the next Corn Dolly champion of the world. You heard it here."

"Tell her that a couple more times," Davey replies.

"One, this is the face of the next Corn Dolly champion of the world. Two, this is . . ."

I shove him away, laughing.

I like being praised by Thom, and then Davey, in this small way. Perhaps there will come a time when I'll think of Gerry and Thom as my friends rather than Davey's friends. They are not people I would ever have met in Otters Holt.

Inside Pizza Pans, we order two pies with entire gardens buried under cheese. I'm picking off spinach when I see Thom take a hairpin from behind Gerry's ear and fasten it to his folded napkin. Ceremoniously, he presents me with "Napkin Dolly, 2017" and says, "I hereby declare Billie McCaffrey to be deserving of this Napkin Dolly based purely upon . . ." He looks at Gerry. "What's it based purely upon, my love?"

Gerry says, "Soul brightness," and Thom is happy to insert this into his speech.

"Based purely upon soul brightness. Now mount this table"—he smacks it with his palm, rattling the dishes and splashing water from the glasses—"and give us all a speech."

"Is he serious?" I ask Davey.

"Afraid so."

I surreptitiously check to see how much everyone has eaten. We will be asked to leave Pizza Pans and I don't want to leave Gerry hangry. Picking up Napkin Dolly, 2017, I climb from floor to chair to table, and plant my boots near the parmesan cheese shakers and the red pepper flakes. Gerry, Davey, and Thom bang their utensils in unison. "Speech, Speech, Speech."

My head is almost lodged in a light fixture. Our waiter says, "Miss, miss, you can't be up there. You have to—" when I open my mouth and sing one line from that *Dirty Dancing* song about having the time of my life. This is all the invitation Gerry needs. She's on her chair. Thom and Davey follow. I lift the Napkin Dolly for the restaurant to see, and we sing—quite terribly—every word we know and don't know.

Fifteen seconds of fame before the manager appears.

Money is exchanged—Thom to manager. We all land in the parking lot laughing our heads off. Thom tells me, "That was a lovely exit strategy, but I missed your acceptance speech."

I hold the napkin, which is back in its former state as Gerry reclaimed her hairpin, and say, "I hereby accept this Napkin Dolly and all the rights and privileges pertaining thereto."

Thom gives me a flourish. "Because . . ."

"Because you gave her to me," I add.

"Because you are worthy," he says.

"Based on soul brightness," Davey says.

I'm chuffed. It's silly, but being bestowed a Napkin Dolly touches me.

We are walking to our cars. Davey is with Thomas. Gerry has claimed me. We are looped together, our elbows hooked like chain-link fencing. Her doing. Not mine. They promise that they will come to Otters Holt soon. We swear we'll be back.

Gerry says, "We're all doing the LaserCon thing, yeah?"

Davey peers over his shoulder, eyebrows raised with questions. *Can I do what I said? Did I mean it?*

He senses my immediate willingness.

"Yesssssssssssss!" he yells at the shadow of the Batman building. There's no time to be astonished. Gerry jumps, lifting me off the sidewalk. Suddenly we're all jumping and yesssssing like lunatics.

I don't really even know why. I just liked that first long yes from Davey, head bent nearly horizontal, and the top of his bandanna showing. Handsome and happy, dancing and spinning top-like through the street. Thom, who has slung his arm around Davey's back, whispers something I cannot hear. Something that makes Davey howl at the moon.

"What do you know of them?" Gerry asks me, also in a whisper.

"Only that they love each other."

And I wonder if she knows when I say *love*, that I mean the kind of love that probably excludes her. And me.

I'm still thinking of love when we're in the Camaro and the city is behind us. "Will you tell me more about Thom? About you and Thom?" This seems a fair exchange. I told him about my sex dream. About Janie Lee. About kissing Woods.

But Davey bristles. Volcano Choir is on the radio. I've just told my parents I'll be home by nine. It's looking more like nine thirty, which I knew when I said nine. I'm remembering Thom's words to me during dinner. Before the karaoke, when we were both still dazed from the afternoon. As Davey slunk lizard-like toward the men's room, Thom said to me, "Keep a watch on our boy."

What specifically was I to watch? He'd moved. Lost his grandfather. Lost his father. Been hurled into culture shock. Thom was clearly sharing Davey with me, but I thought maybe he assumed Davey had told me more than he had. I wanted to *keep a watch*, but there wasn't time to ask, "For what?"

I began with what I knew, greasing the track. "He's really great. Is it hard for you to see him with Gerry?"

"Billie. I think you've gotten this wrong."

"I'm just saying, you can talk to me. I'll still like them both."

"Which costume should we build for LaserCon?" he asks.

I barrel forward with the previous conversation. "I get it. I promise I do. I mean . . . you *know* I do, what with Woods and Janie Lee. And I'll bet you had a lot more freedom in Nashville than in Otters Holt."

He knuckles the wheel. And then the gearshift. And then

his thigh. "I'm thinking something classic. Maybe old Marvel. Or old Disney."

"But even if you had freedom at Waylan, that doesn't mean your parents are cool." I am remembering Dad's voice from the dinner table, and how Hattie needs to come to coffee with my mom because she's upset. "Like I know I could come out in the Hexagon if I wanted to, but at home, that would never be an easy conversation. Never an easy life. If I followed that path into the future, my dad would never come to my wedding. Mom probably would. But Dad, never."

"How do you feel about Iron Man?" Davey's poker face is amazing. "Or Wolverine?"

"It's hard to know the consequences in advance. Hard to have the freedom to still choose when you know how all the pieces in the game will behave if you do."

He stays to his path. "Iron Man will probably be overdone. Disney is better. What if we did a duo? Would you think on an interesting duo? Something creative that will stand out?"

"I just needed to say that. To say, you can talk to me if you want."

"Maybe Beauty and the Beast. Would you like that? If we win the money, you can have it all. It's a thousand bucks."

"I love Beauty and the Beast," I say.

"Good talk," he says.

I know he heard me.

20

Davey's Part

It started with a phone call. Woods Carrington had never called me before. Group text, yes. Voice in an actual receiver, no.

He jumped straight to the point, saving his idle chit-chat for people collecting Social Security. "I need your help, Davey."

I'd been giving him help nearly every morning at 6:45 a.m. What else could he possibly need?

"Meet me at the Fork and Spoon tomorrow morning before school? Six thirty?"

I'd said yes and yes, because people do not tell Woods no. They don't even tell Woods they'll think about it.

"Bring Big T's Bible."

It was a peculiar ask, but I showed up at 6:10, Bible under my arm, and found him tapping his foot in the vestibule, as if I was late. Janie Lee was standing in the corner looking amped. They didn't explain our objective, but they'd clearly discussed it with each other, and from the body language, he thought it would work, she didn't. They saw the Bible, Woods said, "Good work, Winters," and in we went.

There in the middle of the Fork and Spoon was a long wooden table, covered in sunny yellow coffee mugs and eggs cooked hard to runny. A little wooden sign read *The Liars Table*. There sat ten Otters Holtians, who gathered daily to natter and chatter their morning away. Woods was the only one under the age of Depends who had a regular seat. Some guys played video games and scrolled their phones; Woods Carrington sipped coffee and collected stories. His vernacular here included: "Don't you go throwing a hip," and "You been kickin' back too much Ensure?" and "You do that again, and I'll take you to the home myself."

I saw it all play out as he made the rounds; they loved him like a mascot.

I have a vague memory of Big T bringing me to this same table, propping me on his knee, and ordering us two Cokes. He'd take a pen from the breast pocket of his polo and tell me to color in the O's on the paper place mat while he chewed the fat with a few folks.

Janie Lee sat down next to Woods while I stole a chair

from a nearby table and coughed at the smoke billowing from an adjoining room. This must be the one restaurant in the state where you could still smoke indoors. Or maybe you can't and they did it anyway.

I ordered some diesel from a waitress who was probably here when Big T ordered those Cokes years before. I was in my usual attire, so one of the ladies grunted, and another sneered. I was with Woods, so they kept it kinder than they would if I were alone.

Billie's grandma was there. She said, "These young people have been up cracking the whip. You should see the elementary school, Abram," and a lady down the table said, "We know, Clarissa."

Abram gave me a wink, as if we had a secret. "Oh, I've motored by there a time or two. Looking mighty nice, kids."

I didn't actually think he'd seen the elementary school yet, but he wanted Grandy to think he had. His teeth were big crooked squares, all tobacco-stained. He reminded me of Big T. I tweaked my mouth and swallowed some emotion.

I exchanged a fitful look with Woods, and he said, "The elementary school was all Davey's idea."

I shrugged. "The elementary school's history is tied to the festival. It would have made Big T proud." This was an easy thing to say because it was the truth.

"Honestly, Mr. Jones"—Abram's last name—"don't we owe it to Big T's memory to make this the best Harvest Festival ever?" Woods said.

Janie Lee added her own fuel. "I think we owe it to his memory to never let it stop."

"It does seem a shame to let a wonderful thing die," a lady with one of those trach voice boxes whispered.

Another woman, much plumper than the first, death-gripped her coffee and said, "Plus, there's Molly. We can't rightly have a statue without the festival. Just feels wrong."

I couldn't keep up with the banter that followed. Some agreed. Some disagreed. The fact remained that the Harvest Festival is expensive, and no one is sure how to change that.

Woods retrieved a saltshaker from the center of the table, slid it back and forth in a soothing rhythm. "Ada May, if you ask me, I think you've got a golden opportunity with the ballots."

"You're a sly pup, Woodsey Woodsey, but we're not telling you who we've chosen," said Wilma Frost.

Woods gave Wilma a handsome but overbearing wink. "I'm not asking you to tell me you've chosen Tawny Jacobs again, darlin'. I'm asking you to work with me. I've got a plan to save this thing, money and all, but I need your help."

"Yeah, we need your help," Janie Lee said.

I watched the plump lady and the lady with the trach have another conversation and overheard, "Is that the Miller girl?"

Woods shut that down. "Ada May, you and the committee should give the town something to talk about." Woods slid the Bible slightly toward them. "And you know who thought of this idea?"

"Thought of what idea?" Wilma asked.

"The next round of nominees. Or *a* nominee," Janie Lee supplied.

I was not sure what Woods and Janie Lee had dragged me into, but it was interesting. To my knowledge, Woods had never perused Big T's King James, so whatever he was playing at, he had to hope they took the bait without asking for evidence.

Wilma stroked her blouse, both offended and interested. "You're saying Big T wrote someone he wanted nominated for this year's Corn Dolly in his King James? Because he never spoke hide nor hair of it to me."

Woods tapped the worn leather right on the golden embossed letters of Tyson Vilmer's name. "Right there in the book of Luke."

"And who did he have in mind?" Abram asked.

Woods looked at Grandy and then at me. "Elizabeth McCaffrey."

The table was silent. My brain cranked to life. Now I saw. I imagined a conversation that happened between Janie Lee and Woods after he so stupidly put Billie on the guys' side of the Hexagon.

We're idiots, he might have said.

Huge ones, she might have agreed.

But I'll fix this, he would have said.

And then he came up with this plan to take Billie from tomboy to best woman in town, ignoring the fact that Billie would not appreciate this campaign.

Ada May started to say, "And didn't Billie catch Community Ch—" but Grandy would hear nothing negative about her granddaughter.

"An accident. Nothing more," Grandy snapped.

Abram added his two cents. "But what's not an accident is all the hard work the youth have been doing in the community. Think on that, Ada May."

Wilma talked over Ada May. "Please, Abram. Several weeks of work do not a Corn Dolly candidate make. This has to be a woman of valor or the whole thing loses its intention."

"It takes heart," someone else said.

"Which my granddaughter has in spades."

This brought the conversation circling back to the King James. Janie Lee said, "And heart is precisely why Tyson wrote Elizabeth McCaffrey's name down as the next nominee."

Woods lifted the Bible from the table and placed the evidence in his lap. "Come on, Ada May, it's good for the town. We've never had a teenage girl on the ballot before. Bring some new life to the festival. People will respond. They'll remember why it's important. They'll donate. We'll kill two birds with one stone."

Sometimes a seed goes into rock-hard clay in a barren

desert. And sometimes it falls into manure and sunlight beside the grandness of Kentucky Lake.

Ada May had the last word. It's not what she said, but how she said it. Ears open. Heart soft. "The committee will take your suggestion under advisement."

Woods threw his arms around the back of my and Janie Lee's chairs, binding us together in this scheme. He smiled because he knew that Ada May taking it under advisement was as good as Billie's name on the ballot.

He believed we'd done something good there.

Made up for something lost.

Maybe we did.

But I hope Billie never finds out.

21

I carry myself off to bed around three thirty that night, having spent hours researching Davey's LaserCon. His costumes are all over the home page. Basically, he's a legend. If we're going to win a thousand dollars, Beauty and the Beast will have to be spectacular.

I am so groggy when I get to the elementary school the next morning, I nearly walk right in front of Fifty's mower.

When Janie Lee scoots up next to me and says, "Hey, we're doing our after-school service project together today," I actually groan. I catnap through school, not for the first time, and join Janie Lee in her mother's Acura.

101 Needmore Road, home of Victor Nix, is a white farmhouse half-lost in some untended soybeans. We arrive windblown and delighted by the freedom of a country road.

There's an oak tree in the front yard that must be three hundred years old. It has the remnants of a tree house high in its branches and a dilapidated ladder that doesn't even look safe for squirrels. She parks in its shade and I prop my sunglasses on my head.

"If I fall asleep, punch me," I say.

And then we walk purposefully toward the door and knock. A gentleman, who must have been poised to go out as we were coming in—his trilby hat under his arm, wearing a camel-colored coat with a line of fur that's far too heavy for September—opens the door. "Well, hello there," he says cheerily.

"Mr. Nix?" I greet.

"I am." He raises his neck and shoulders from their slouch, thrilled for company. "And you?"

"I am Billie McCaffrey, and this is Janie Lee Miller. We're out doing some service projects for Community Church, and wanted to see if you needed anything done."

"Well, I was about to run to the mill for seeds, but I guess . . ." He places his key on a hook by the door labeled *Front Door*. "I'm afraid I can't offer you anything fancy to wet your whistle, but I have water from the tap."

Sure that he will give us something to do soon, we accept water in juice glasses and the three of us sit in yellow Naugahyde chairs around a white Formica kitchen table. The clock on the wall chirps like a bird, and a cat emerges from beneath the table and lands on my lap. His tag says *Otis*. He's ogling the selection of Little Debbie cakes in a bowl. Janie Lee is too.

There's a sign on the bowl that reads *Take One. One* is under-lined.

Mr. Nix lifts a chocolate cake. Midair, he passes the cake to Janie Lee. "Did you know my nurse counts these things?"

She eats the cake, which loses me Otis as a friend.

"Mr. Nix, can you think of anything we might help you do?" Janie Lee asks, wadding the paper from the cake and plac-ing it in her pocket.

"Maybe I should check Gloria's list," he says.

Mr. Nix's late wife, Gloria, is the youngest Corn Dolly recipient to date. When she was the fresh age of twenty-three, she won the 1968 Corn Dolly. Though many have tried, no one has replicated the win. Other Corn Dolly winners are all forty and up. When paired with the fact that Mrs. Nix wasn't even mildly attractive, or from a well-reputed family, she's a curios-ity among the aging Corn Dolly queens. (This is discussed and debated freely over coffee and cakes because Gloria Nix died and isn't around to defend herself. She clearly went on living in the heart of Mr. Victor Nix.)

"What did you younguns say you were selling?" Mr. Nix asks, taking a Little Debbie cake from the bowl.

Thinking this man probably needs more company than service, I answer, "We weren't selling anything, sir, but we'd love to hear more about your lovely wife."

"God rest her," Mr. Nix says. "She's over in Fairfield Memo-rial. I need to get some flowers for her grave. Maybe I'll go to the mill later."

Janie Lee sags a little lower in her chair, but says, "We could help you with that."

"Oh, that's so nice," Mr. Nix tells us. "I'm eighty-three. Did you know I don't even have to have a picture on my driver's license anymore?"

From my spot at the table, I have a full view of the front yard. There's no vehicle parked there. No hook labeled *Car Keys* by the door.

"Mr. Nix, would you like us to drive you to the mill?" I suggest.

Mr. Nix pats the part in his hair, and then points a withered finger toward a large shed. "Oh, I must have plenty of seeds in the barn. But I'm not supposed to go out there with my hip." He rubs his left hip, and then his right.

"Mr. Nix, we'll slip out and check. Then we'll help you do some planting for your Gloria."

"Gloria was the most beautiful woman in Otters Holt other than our Hannah," he tells us. And in his old voice, there's a kernel of a much younger voice. I see a woman on tiptoe kissing a smooth-skinned man in the same trilby hat under an oak tree in the front yard.

"Key's around here somewhere." Mr. Nix pats his pockets.

I lift the key off an equally well-labeled hook by the door, and promise we'll be right back with seeds. The door closes behind us. We walk slowly on the path to the shed.

"That man—" Janie Lee says.

"Is painfully wonderful," I finish.

Key to lock, I swing the door wide on its hinges, revealing the shed. There isn't a packet of seeds to retrieve; there are thousands and thousands. Daisies, sunflowers, marigolds. Bins of seeds. Buckets of seeds. Bunches of bulbs. This man has been going to the mill and forgetting he went to the mill for years.

"What do we do?" she asks.

I sink my arms deep in a barrel, let hundreds of prickly bits cling and fall through my fingers. What a wonder. I can't tell whether I am insanely happy at the way he has loved this woman or insanely sad that he hasn't been loved by this woman in so long.

"I think we ask him if we can borrow some seeds for the elementary school," I say.

"Yes," Janie Lee agrees.

First, we load our arms with supplies for Gloria. Flowerpots, soil, Miracle-Gro, and seeds. Inside, we pot the seeds while Mr. Nix searches for Gloria's Corn Dolly. He's intent on showing us, as if we've never seen a Corn Dolly before.

"Mr. Nix, it's okay if you can't find it," I call upstairs.

He is gone long enough that I want to make sure he hasn't fallen, but he returns holding a crumpled Corn Dolly wrapped in a green string of white lights. "With the Christmas stuff," he announces, holding it high above his head, the cord from the lights falling like an unwanted tail. "Gloria liked to use it as an angel."

I take a plate from the cupboard and make peanut butter

sandwiches. "Tell us about the year she won?"

"Oh, yes." He strokes the corn husk carefully and eases his bones into the chair next to mine. They pop audibly. He rubs a hip. "We were astonished she made the ballot. All Tyson Vilmer's doing. Always been a magician. I need to go visit him soon and ask to buy a goat."

Janie Lee flinches and I bite my lip. He continues, "Tyson and Gloria grew up together. Sort of like siblings. It was probably Tyson's influence that made her so strong."

"Is that why she won the Corn Dolly?" I ask.

"Oh, no. It was the flowers."

"The flowers?"

"People were in a rage over Vietnam. Myself as well." He taps the side of his head as if he's wearing a helmet. "And I guess, they just needed happiness instead of war. Gloria wasn't one of those hippie people, but she loved flowers better than anything. Planted them all over town. Mostly without permission. Said to me once, 'Vic'—she always called me Vic instead of Victor—'I can't help myself. I need more color than this.'"

I often feel this way. I like Gloria more and more.

"How many flowers do you think she planted, Mr. Nix?" Janie Lee asks.

"I reckon she did every yard in the county."

Marshall County isn't huge. But the notion of Gloria Nix planting seeds in every yard is huge.

"She was such a pretty soul." His eyes water with love and

memories. He says to Janie Lee, "You are too, dear. What's your name again?"

"Janie Lee," she whispers.

"Mark my words, eyes like that, and you'll be winning your own Corn Dolly one day."

"Thank you, sir. My friend Billie here is on the ballot this year."

"Well, that's wonderful. I didn't understand this dolly hub-bub at first. I says to Gloria, 'There's nothing outright special about a corn husk made into a dolly.' And she says to me, 'Oh, Vic, it's so much more than a doll. It's about being seen.' I must have turned my head halfway around like an owl when she said that. She'd always been something to see, dolly or not, if you asked me."

Grandy's Corn Dolly—Maybel is what she named her—sits beside my Grampy's urn in the pie safe. If there were a fire, Grandy would grab Maybel on the first trip, Grampy on the second. That used to bother me, placing so much value on a thing. But after hearing Mr. Nix, I realize again that the Corn Dolly is not a thing . . . it's a metaphor.

I have been seen in my town, but I've never been seen as Mr. Nix is suggesting. I am not sure I want to be.

The time is seven p.m. And according to the chart beside the Corn Dolly calendar, Mr. Nix is due to shower in thirty minutes.

"You kids are so kind to visit. Let me give you something for your trouble," he says, patting his breast pocket.

I mount a full, but kind, protest. "We won't hear of it. Your company is our payment." This is a line Woods might use at the Liars Table; it is not a lie.

Victor Nix is robotically removing items from the pockets of his coat: Kleenex, money clip, a peppermint, which he offers to Janie Lee and which Janie Lee accepts. Pockets empty, he lifts the camel-colored coat into the air, the way my mom did to me when I was a little girl who wanted to trek into the snow. He coaxes me. "Try it on. Make an old man happy."

"Sir, I can't."

Mr. Nix makes the coat dance. The soft under-skin of his biceps flaps. "Please."

Forced into polite obedience, I try on the man's coat.

Mr. Nix is part tailor, part pixie. He pets the fur collar into submission, makes it lie correctly around my neck. Satisfied, he tugs the lapels and says, "A coat like this might win someone's affection, young man." He nods in Janie Lee's direction, and I wish I hadn't been too tired to attend to myself this morning. Bombshell one day. Man the next.

"Yes, sir," I say.

I leave Mr. Nix's house with my soul in a twist. We don't speak at all on the way to my house and then we speak at the same time.

Janie Lee, who has recovered herself, says, "He knows you're a girl."

And I say, "I think we can transplant all those daylilies to the school."

22

Friday night lights shine high above the football stadium. Insects swarm in little visible clouds even as a cool wind whips through the air, driving up hot chocolate and coffee sales. Davey, Fifty, Mash, and I share a blanket, awaiting the halftime show, in which both Woods and Janie Lee will perform with the band, and I, along with Tawny Jacobs and Caroline Cheatham, will be recognized like homecoming candidates.

Seven minutes left on the clock.

Janie Lee helped me get ready. After Mr. Nix's confusion, I was not surprised this afternoon when she showed up at my house with her overlarge makeup bag and hair accessories. My hair isn't easy to work with. The left side is clipped short. The top is choppy, falling left to right in jutting sections that range from ear-length to chin-length. It's snappy and smart if you're not trying to be sophisticated. The plan is for me to take black dress pants and a blouse—hers, because she insisted—and change just before halftime. Spending an *entire* football game, on cold aluminum bleachers, with concession stand food, in dress clothes? No thank you. This way, I can be back in my jeans as soon as the ceremony is over.

Mash is painted up with school colors—orange and white—and has so much food in his lap that we'll be seeing it a second time around. "Don't eat all that, dude," Fifty tells him.

"What?" Mash protests.

Fifty responds, "You're as likely to throw that up as we are to walk Vilmer's Beam."

"Dude, let it go."

"Do you like football?" I ask Davey while the other two duke shit out.

Mash speaks around the hot dog. "You played football at Waylan, yeah?"

Davey seems interested in something happening to the band. They're assembling on the track, thirty feet below. I know better than to show him sympathy with Fifty around. He answers his cousin reluctantly, "Yes, and lacrosse."

John Winters is on his way up the bleachers. Beneath the blanket, Davey squeezes my knee.

Halfway to us, John stops. "David." He gives a quick wave.

"Can you see my makeup?" Davey asks me.

In truth, better than usual. Heavier eyeliner and a tiny

bit of smoky gray shadow. That isn't the response he wants. I uncoil fingers from my knee, and whisper the easiest truth, "He's seen you in costumes before."

"But not at football games," Davey says.

Five minutes left on the clock before halftime. I need to go change, but . . . I need to be here more.

"David," John Winters calls again.

Davey removes himself from the blanket and goes. He's wearing a shredded band shirt, bright-blue skinny jeans, black Converse high tops, and more glue in his hair than a kindergartner after an art class. This outfit causes John Winters to frown, and then set his jaw with fury. John must decide he needs a better look at Davey's friends because Davey returns to us under the arm of his father.

Before they arrive, Fifty says, "Dude's a prick," and Mash says, "You have no idea."

John makes room for himself on our bench. We fall under his scrutiny. He nods at Mash and to the rest of us he says, "Hello, townie friends."

No one speaks.

I assume he is a man used to pivoting around uncomfortable situations, because he gestures to the crowd and says, "What do you think of all this hubbub over a cornstalk?"

Four minutes left on the clock.

Fifty scratches a sideburn, answers, "We think it's fucking delightful, sir."

Oh my God, I love Fifty right now.

Mash chokes on his hot dog, and I slap him hard on the back. He spits hot dog and ketchup and bun all over my jeans. "God, I'm sorry," he says to me, using a slimy napkin to remove the damage. If I'm going to change, I need to leave right now.

John folds robotic arms over his puffy chest, blocks the end of our bench. "David, I want to know what's so *fucking delightful* that your friend here would say that to his elder."

For Davey's sake, I try to schmooze. "I believe Fifty is just excited because I'm on the ballot this year?"

"You?"

I start to stand, wiping at the smudgy places on my jeans.

"Your mother was on that stage once," John informs Davey. Davey doesn't react. It's new information to me. They don't put nominees on the Corn Dolly calendar, only the winners. John tells us, "I stood right over there and listened to Big Bad Tyson Vilmer read a paragraph on her worthiness. As if baking pies and planting flowers and nursing babies will get you anywhere. That's when I knew I had to get her out of here."

Three minutes on the clock.

We are all wriggling, no one more so than Davey. "You should have black-out under your eyes, not around them," he tells Davey. "I talked to your lacrosse coach. He says if you come back to Waylan in the spring, he won't penalize you for not starting the season with the team." Davey says nothing at John's continued commentary. "You can't possibly want to throw away scholarship offers."

This isn't a conversation for public consumption.

Two minutes on the clock. Nominees are moving down the bleachers. The stage gets wheeled to the track. The band members have assembled at the urging of the director. I should go change right now.

John Winters fills the air with more arguments. "You seem pretty satisfied with all this nothingness. Which is why I told Thomas I'd trade him my Mustang if he got you to come back to Waylan."

This is too much. "You didn't," Davey says.

"I've only got one son. And I'd like to see him make something of himself." He licks his thumb, as if Davey is five, and makes a show of smearing Davey's makeup in front of us.

Davey is stock-still.

I wrestle with not punching John Winters. Fifty might be too lazy to do most things, but he has no intention of backing down, elder or not.

"I don't think anyone here has any interest in hearing you speak again," Fifty tells John.

One minute on the clock.

I can't keep myself from quietly asking Davey, "Would you really move back with him?"

He tells me, "I might have to."

The clock ticks down. Halftime. And I am not dressed. And I have been spit up on. All of Otters Holt stands and claps as the Otters run to the locker room. The stadium is overfull and bubbling with anticipation. Every generation in town has turned up to see the halftime show: the Liars Table, the

Methodists, the Baptists, the Corn Dolly committee, Corn Dolly winners of old (they have their own section and sashes), football parents, band parents, everyone. Even Mr. Nix and his nurse. They're all on their feet. They're all a force.

Only John Winters sits.

"You need to go, Billie," Mash says. "They're waving at you."

While we've been having this chat, the band has taken the field, and two stages that were poised on the track have been wheeled to the fifty-yard line. Janie Lee and Woods are atop one, mic'd and ready to perform in conjunction with the band at the conductor's command. Woods is wearing a sweater that does him no favors. Cable-knit. If it didn't have the wooden toggle buttons, the whole thing could be repurposed for a rag, and yet he is still very good-looking. Janie Lee is even better still.

Fifty hollers, "Yeah, Woodsey! Yeah, Janie!"

The field commander climbs onto her box, flips her wrists. Brass and flutes and drums are everywhere. The first feat: Someone creative has ripped the explicit words from "Starships." The second: The band has moves. The third: Janie Lee and Woods dance and sing on their stage as if they own the field.

"*Damn*," Fifty says.

"Go," Davey says. "I'll be fine."

He says this, but he's drawn up, distant, other.

Mash nudges me. Nods at John. "What do we do about him?"

I say, "I. Do. Not. Know."

We both wish Woods were here. But he is on the stage, right hand lifted in a final note. Around him, the color-guard flags slow to a stop. The band's horns are all lifted and gleaming under the stadium lights. Everyone applauds. Woods and Janie Lee bow. The band breaks into the fight song to file off the field.

And now I must go. I can wait no longer. I have to entrust Davey to Mash and Fifty.

Tawny Jacobs and Caroline Cheatham stand, fidgeting and nervous, behind Ada May Adcock, Rebecca Carnicky, Wilma Frist, and several other committee members. They are all looking frantic that I'm not there. Here is what is supposed to happen: the mayor will say something about each of us and we will step forward and wave and then step back. It sounded very manageable when I read the mailed instructions from the mayor's office. The same instructions that said Sunday-best attire was suggested but not required.

I perform a stadium check. Where is my dad? My mom? How furious will they be when I walk out on that stage in dirty jeans and an orange Otters Holt sweatshirt?

I reach Ada May and apologize. "I had an accident," I have only managed to say when she whirls me around to face the crowd.

We are three women. Three generations. Who are supposed to be perfect specimens. Tawny in her pearls to my left. Caroline to my right in her diamonds. My competitors are draped in expensive clothes, are trimmed with et cetera, and I think, *Women are made of et cetera.*

Our mayor, a stout, well-respected man with a nose the shape of a lightbulb, holds the microphone. He reads about Tawny, long sweeping paragraphs about her financial generosity and kind demeanor that everyone knows is bullshit. Then he reads about Caroline, who is the poet laureate of Kentucky and a retired lieutenant colonel in the Army.

I'm next. Feeling ridiculous, I step forward, wave. He reads: "Elizabeth McCaffrey is the daughter of local minister Scott McCaffrey and local artist Clare McCaffrey. She is a third-generation McCaffrey to attend Otters Holt High School. She is the first teenager in the history of Otters Holt to be nominated for a Corn Dolly."

That's it. People are polite enough to clap. Including my parents, but they wear bewildered faces, either from his short paragraph or my clothes.

He didn't mention rescuing Janie Lee from the water moccasin or the recent service projects. Perhaps because I was late. Perhaps because the person in charge of writing them isn't my fan. Instead, I am a blazing example of why Woods put me on the guys' side of the Hexagon. Hair tangled. Clothes rumpled. Hot dog chunks on my jeans.

He pets the air, begging the crowd to pipe down. "As you've probably guessed, with the passing of our benefactor, this year will be the last Harvest Festival. So the last awarded Corn Dolly will go to one of these ladies." Whether it is planned for effect or he's momentarily overcome, he pauses, keeps pausing, keeps pausing, says, "Let's make sure it's the best one yet."

A pattering, polite as a golf crowd, moves through the bleachers. The mayor disappears like a referee after a terrible ballgame. The platforms are wheeled away by a high school crew.

The football team returns to a quiet stadium.

23

At halftime, a swarm of people are gossiping and searching for another bag of popcorn. All around me, the old tell the very young they are "sorry" and the young ask the old, "For what?" Many of them, like the John Winterses of the world, don't understand the joy of eating roasted corn row-on-row or the pleasure of savoring Mrs. Rankin's pumpkin-flavored lollipops to the last lick. The very young haven't danced "Sally Down the Alley" or the "Potta Potta" or stayed up watching a movie on the side of Vilmer's Barn. The very young don't know the crescendo of emotions when a woman climbs three stage steps and accepts the Corn Dolly.

In my mind, I taste, I dance, I watch, I swell with memories. I am nostalgic for a future where I will have done all these things for decades.

I am not very young.

I am also in trouble.

Dad invites me into a makeshift office under the bleachers. We are among the bubble gum wrappers and dropped popcorn and paper cups. The throwaway things. Directly above us are the Corn Dolly winners. They are talking about me. Some using the word *disgrace*, others *modern*. Unaware that we are beneath them, one says, "I don't see how Scott McCaffrey can control a congregation when he lets his daughter run all over him."

"Do you even go to Community Church?" someone asks.

The accuser says, "No." She says *No* as if to say *Why would I?*

Dad and I are frozen, listening for the next comment, but some football thing happens and cheers drown out the discussion. Dad points upward and gives me a face. The this-is-what-I'm-talking-about face. And I try to give him a face too. *Just because they're talking . . . are they right?* His hands dive deep in his pockets; I get a view of his chin. A long view. As he prays or decides what to say first.

"What happened?" he asks.

A level question. The benefit of doubt.

Rather than explain, I say, "Nothing you'll believe."

"Try me."

When I reach for explanations, they are not there. He is furious and ashamed of my behavior, but he hugs me anyway. I am pressed against him, his arms circle my back, we twist in a tiny swaying arc of love. I am inside his jacket, the silky lining soft and warm on my arms. I do not cry; I am numb with disappointment.

I tell him what happened. How John Winters showed up and I couldn't leave Davey. How my gut was ringing and singing that being there was more important than dressing up. But that I did have dress clothes hanging in the girls' bathroom. That I even had lipstick in my pocket. Bright red that could be seen from the top of the stands.

"It'll be okay," he tells me.

But we both know the words are as empty as the cups that have fallen from above.

Behind us, Coach Tilghman, Fifty's uncle, barks, "Hustle up!" and "Come on, defense!" at his players. The scoreboard changes by three points. Above us the crowd watches and follows the cheerleaders' prompts. "Give me an O! Give me a T!" But I doubt they have forgotten the halftime show. They will take to landlines. Sit in booths at the Fork and Spoon. Gather on porches, in cars and church pews, by newspaper stands, and they will "discuss" with vigor the faults of Elizabeth McCaffrey. It is easy to speculate, because it is a repeating piece of history. Some will blame my parents. Some will blame my youth. Some will blame the modern age. But they will blame.

"I love living here and I hate living here," I whisper.

Dad puts a finger under my chin. He looks directly into my eyes. He says, not sweetly, not firmly, but somewhere in between, "You did your best. Anytime you can promise me, 'Dad, that was my best,' it'll always be enough for me. If we move, we move."

Three hours later, he will forget what he has said.

24

Davey's Part

A phone conversation between David Winters and Thomas Cahill after the football game.

THOMAS: You don't sound good.

DAVID: Thom, if I tell you something, will you promise not to laugh?

THOMAS: No. But I promise I'll stop eventually.

DAVID: You know the Harvest Festival?

THOMAS: The one your Octagon is working to save? The one you talk about all the frickin' time?

DAVID: Hexagon.

THOMAS: Parallelogram. Rhombus. I'll stop.

DAVID: Thank you.

THOMAS: What's going on now?

DAVID: It's stupid.

THOMAS: When has that ever stopped you before?

DAVID: When I was a kid, maybe six or seven, Big T took me to the festival.

THOMAS: Nostalgia is not stupid. What's that Santayana quote? "Those who do not remember the past are condemned to repeat it."

DAVID: I can hear you googling.

THOMAS: I want to make sure I said it right. Keep talking.

DAVID: My parents went to the festival. I have all these vague fond memories. Playing Wiffle ball. Meeting a girl in a Batman costume. I even have this memory of my parents dancing. They might not have been happy, but in my head, they still loved each other then. They met at the Harvest Festival. Evidently, in college, my dad owned a couple of those inflatable bouncy things and rented them out to make money.

THOMAS: Sounds like him.

DAVID: And I know it's childish, but if it ends—

THOMAS: You'll lose your parents again.

DAVID: No. It's not so much them. It's that a piece of the place I came from will be gone. Does that make sense?

THOMAS: I want to hear more. By the way, the quote is right.

DAVID: Of course it is. Anyway, my grandfather invested so much in the festival, because he thought it brought people together. And I guess, even though my parents aren't a great fit, and my dad is a total d-bag, I feel . . . I don't know . . . a sense of responsibility.

THOMAS: That's deep, Winters.

DAVID: I'm thinking about making a donation, but I know it'll piss my dad off.

THOMAS: What doesn't piss your dad off?

DAVID: If I do it, I'm not sure . . . I'm not sure if we can come back from it. It'll be a betrayal.

THOMAS: Why don't you wait and see if you win LaserCon?

DAVID: True.

THOMAS: That way you don't necessarily have to burn the bridge with your dad.

DAVID: Good point.

THOMAS: You're fighting awfully hard to stay there.

DAVID: Unexpectedly, yes.

THOMAS: *Happy in Podunk*, a memoir by David Winters.

DAVID: Don't call it Podunk.

THOMAS: I've been waiting months for you to tell me that.

DAVID: (Laughs)

THOMAS: What can I do to help Save. The. Festival?

DAVID: How do you feel about kickball?

THOMAS: Like I'm on my way to Otters Holt right now.

DAVID: No, seriously.

THOMAS: I was serious. Name the time and the place.

DAVID: Saturday after LaserCon.

THOMAS. Consider it done. Hey, you told Billie the truth
about the Corn Dolly stuff yet?

DAVID: No.

THOMAS: Clock's ticking.

DAVID: I know. I know.

25

I shower off the hot dog and humiliation and retreat to the garage to flatten some aluminum cans with a mallet.

Janie Lee is turning the screws on the bow of her violin, tightening the hairs to practice. When they are perfectly taut, she applies the rosin. I like to watch her complete this methodical process. It is the most disciplined thing she does, and has always told me so much about her.

She followed me home from the game like a puppy. We didn't discuss the concern in her eyes, but I saw it there, leaning toward me like a conversation. "I don't need to talk about it," I said as I hung her borrowed clothes from the handle above the backseat window. But she probably *did* need to talk about it. Because any time I am not fine, or she thinks I am not fine, it pecks at her like a chicken.

She plays the sad, lonely notes from Tchaikovsky's Violin Concerto in D Major.

To make matters worse, she wears the same clothes from the night of the fire—the dream clothes. Pajamas and flannel and lips I tried to kiss off her face.

Elizabeth McCaffrey, born 1999—d. ? IN LOVING MEMORY: Murdered by UGGs.

These feelings need sorting. *Just friends is better,* I think.

I am capable of mind-over-mattering anything. For instance . . . these cans. They were round beverage holders. Nearly forty of them have gone under my X-Acto knife and lie like thin sheets of aluminum paper on the worktable, ready to be Guinevere's breastplate. After I make this, I will move on to the Beauty and the Beast costumes Davey says will win us a thousand dollars. The supplies are set up on the far wall. Maybe I'll start tonight after Janie Lee goes home.

One long note rises from the violin. It is not part of a known song. I stop flattening the cans. "What is it?" I ask.

She cuts big clear eyes toward the driveway, toward something unseen. "I was just thinking about you standing up there tonight," she says.

The aluminum can is as flat as my mallet will make it. "I was a disaster."

"You weren't," she insists. "You were just yourself. The mayor was an asshole."

We battle eye on eye, me knowing that if I say, *Me being myself is the problem,* then she has a best friend obligation to dispute me. Something sugary and sweet like, *Woods and I thought you were perfect.* Which A) discounts the praise entirely, and B) is utter bullshit.

"Regardless of what the mayor said, I looked awful."

"You didn't."

I skip this praise too. "I was worried about Davey. His dad, man, he's a ruckus." *Ruckus* is the nicest word in my vocabulary for John Winters. "I couldn't make myself go and get ready."

"Fifty told me. Said Davey's dad is pressuring him to move back to Nashville."

"Yeah."

She looks uncertain. She asks, "How will you feel about that?"

"I'll miss him."

Davey is Hexagon, but he does not specifically belong to her the way it feels that he does to me. She is sad on my behalf, but it only stretches so far. "Are you going to kiss him?" she asks.

Her fingertips idly touch the hair on her bow, so I'm aware that she's very unfocused. She is very methodical about the oils in her skin and their relationship to all things violin.

I am honest with her. "I would like to. You know, just to see if anything is there. I'm not even sure if he's available."

"I have people like that."

That's when my heart starts its galloping. Pieces of the dream, ones that had drifted hazily away, come punching back to reality.

"You know the day of the Hexagon of Love?" she asks.

I set the mallet away. "Sure," I say.

"I know you were hurt about Woods putting you on the guys' side, but did you notice anything else?"

What else was there to notice? Woods picking Mary Dancy? Old news. He does not, nor did he ever like her, and we both know that. This was either a diversionary tactic or cowardly action. I remind her of this, and she plays three lines of a Lindsey Stirling song she's been obsessing over. Then she says, "Did you see our names? How it almost looked like they matched?"

I take my mallet back. Banging it against the cans, over and over, I consider my options. To answer is to take a flying leap into dangerous territory. Her shirt is blue, and I am noticing that her eyes are bluer right now than they were when she was dressed up earlier. She is noticing I am not answering her.

With the larger end of the violin, she pokes my stomach. "McCaffrey?"

"Yeah, I saw," I admit.

"And what did it make you think?"

She is opening a door. We both hear the hinges squeak. She told me a week ago that *just friends is better*. What has changed other than me wearing upchucked hot dog in front of the whole town? Nothing. And pity is a terrible reason to kiss someone you love.

I flatten my voice, remove every trace of passion like I am sweeping the corner of a dusty room. "I was pretty upset about the whole you're-a-dude thing. I didn't think about much else."

With Woods, we decided to kiss the way we decided we would save the Harvest Festival or blow up a sock. Thoughtfully, strategically, antiseptically. It was simple because it was always somewhere I knew I might land. With Janie Lee, this is all so new. There are other barriers. Do we really want to go there? Risk changing the fundamental nature of our friendship? She isn't Gerry. I'll have to see her regularly. There could be residue if this shakes out poorly. And do two names, across from each other on Einstein, mean anything?

As far as she knows, I'm buying a hundred acres beneath Molly the Corn Dolly and living here until I have an actual tombstone. She specifically cited future plans in another city as a reason things with Woods wouldn't work out. By her own ideals, I am a bad choice. Why do this now?

But I know why. We're curious. I'm fixated on the idea of *What if?* We may never get another moment when we are this open. And although I am afraid it will change us, Woods and I are doing just fine. Courage begets courage.

"All right, Miller. Let's do this thing," I say.

Neither of us needs a definition. She does not give me a chance to change my mind. In a familiar way, she moves closer, pushes the mallet until it falls off the table and bounces under the saw. She twirls a piece of my hair around her finger.

I duplicate her action, touching her hair, and then her earlobe. She's always touching, petting, stroking, and cuddling. I am none of these things.

The moment to bail arrives. She stares at my hand, aware. Stares at my mouth, aware. The tip of her tongue is poised on her bottom lip. The violin hangs between us. History is between us too.

"Billie?" My name is a question.

I carefully slip the bow and violin away and set them behind us. Her UGGs bump against my boots; her fingers, still tangled in my hair, touch my earlobe, once, twice, three times. "You love me," I say, because that part of us is not in question.

Her cheeks are flushed. Mine must be too.

"I don't know how I love you, only that I do, and I can't not," she says.

"Me too," I say quietly.

My face is against her hand now. I am not the one who moved. I am not the one who has her thumb on my cheek.

"Kiss me?" I say, choosing to only move my boot a fraction closer to her.

I want her to make this choice so I will not look back at this moment and feel as though it was forced. And unlike Woods, she breaks the barrier between us first.

I am being kissed.

It is mostly mouth and no tongue—a quartet of lips and softness. She is all melody. My job is to harmonize. I hear the Irish ballad Davey played on the way home from Nashville. She has a merry and somber mouth. Just like the music.

We are still kissing.

I compare her to Gerry. Gerry kisses like the world

will end soon. Janie Lee kisses like the world was born this morning.

We are still kissing.

I am living a moment the Spandex Junkwagons have gossiped about. That my father fears. That scares me. A lightning bolt from heaven doesn't strike.

I am okay. I am grateful.

I am trembling. I am praying.

It is me who breaks away. Me who wipes her spit from my mouth.

Her fingers are stuck in her pockets; her hair is stuck to her lip. Casual as ever, I tuck it behind her ear. She half-grins, and rubs her cheek against her shoulders as if she can clean the red from her cheeks. Then she is busy dusting garage molecules from her violin and returning it to the case.

"Are you okay?" I ask.

Someone clears a throat.

It is not me. It is not Janie Lee.

26

Dad and Tawny Jacobs stand at the open door of our garage, arms burdened with newspapers—a donation for the Daily Sit, promised the day I picked pecans on her farm. It was a kindness I had not expected her to offer. Certainly not one I predicted would arrive at ten thirty p.m. on the Friday night I was kissing a girl.

She must have parked in the circle drive out front while I was malleting.

She says nothing. Bless her. After lowering her stack of newspapers to the couch, she says, "See you Sunday, Brother Scott," and dismisses herself. I hear her pull onto River Run Road over the sound of me kicking my own ass.

I also swear I can hear my father's heart banging against his rib cage from across the garage.

He collapses on the steps leading inside, hands steepled, fingertips stroking the bridge of his nose. The rest of him is immobile. Janie Lee looks at me.

"I think you'd better go home," he tells her.

It is amazing she didn't say this herself. Amazing she didn't run screaming away.

Her violin case appears to weigh forty million pounds. Pausing at the garage door, she mouths, "I'm sorry," and I hope she means for being caught, but I am unsure. When she reaches the end of the drive, Dad presses the lit orange button above his shoulder, lowering the garage door, trapping us.

I am bathed in fluorescent light and humility.

He's wearing fur moccasins he keeps on the rug by the front door for errands. They make no sound on the three wooden steps or the concrete. Made no sounds on the sidewalk earlier. If he'd been wearing his wing tips, I would have heard him.

Five steps. He crosses the garage and stoops to pick up the mallet and sets it on my worktable, as if returning at least one thing to order will help. When he arrives before me, I flinch as though he might strike. He does nothing with his outstretched hands. They stay between us like he means to lay hands on me and pray.

My own arms are limp celery, falling at my sides. I squeeze the fabric of my athletic pants, work it between my fingers, waiting on judgment.

He sniffs, and I can't keep myself from saying, "Dad, it's not what—"

"I don't care what it was."

His tone is even, which is worse than if it were rageful.

"We—"

"Stop. I need to think." A tear hangs on his chin. "I've put up with ridiculous schemes. Footballs in the sanctuary. Church fires. But this, this is . . . something else. And Tawny . . ." He groans. Props himself against the freezer, body shaped like a C, unseeing. "You *know*. You know things at church are precarious. You know we're under a microscope."

"Dad, you can't think I could have known that you and Tawny would walk in right then. That wasn't about you or church."

"Billie, that's what I'm saying. You can't predict anything. I asked you, I specifically asked you, to rein it in."

I nod that I understand.

The warning continues. "I think you just bought us a one-way ticket out of town."

"Dad—"

"If Tawny takes what she saw public, I can't get you out of this."

I am grasping at straws. "What about the Corn Dolly? What if I turn it around?"

He laughs. *Please don't laugh*, I think. *This is my life*, I think.

My cell buzzes from across the room. It must be Janie Lee.

I want to tell him I love Janie Lee. That I always will. But that I have not had enough experience to trust my heart. That I still want to kiss Davey, who wants to kiss Thom, who is probably somewhere kissing Gerry. That I am hopelessly confused.

I am open. I am closed. I am terrified. It comes out like: "Dad, I'm not pursuing Janie Lee—"

"No, you're not."

"You're forbidding me?"

He exhales. "No, I'm begging you, for once in your life, to think about someone other than yourself. Do you hear me?"

I kissed her. I think I would kiss her again, but . . . I'm not sure. As much as I wanted this thing to happen, I wasn't prepared to enjoy it that much *and* feel so uncertain at the same time.

"I hear you," I say.

I hear that he has dumped a landfill worth of guilt on me. I hear myself shrinking to the size of my boots when I was just eighty feet tall a moment ago.

The cell buzzes again.

Dad examines my intentions. I have no idea what is there for his viewing pleasure.

He tries to soften his blows. "Honey, this is not about whether you love her. Your mother and I have always known you might choose . . ." There's a pregnant pause. ". . . differently from us. But this isn't about your sexuality, this is about stability and sensibility in the moment." He wipes his nose with his index finger. At the door to the house, he grips the doorframe and says, "I love you, but Billie, for the love of God, cool your jets."

My mind is a filing cabinet full of things I should not say.

"Okay," I agree.

"Okay," he says.

We've struck a deal without a handshake.

THE SHORT PART

before

PART THREE

I know what I have given you. I do not know what you have received.

—ANTONIO PORCHIA

Whenever David's teacher asked him to draw a picture of his home, he drew Big T's instead.

His grandfather's house was a maze of interesting things, and nearly none of them was breakable. There were wooden bunk beds in the guest room, fields and barns to play in, and a library with so many books David needed a ladder to reach them all. But better than bunk beds and coffee table books about fighter planes was Big T himself.

David wasn't the only one who thought so, because Big T had his very own festival. And everyone in town came out to celebrate. According to Big T, there was cotton candy and roasted corn and dunking booths. There were games and square dancing and ceremonies. There was fun and fun and more fun.

This sounded like a grand fairy tale or something David had read in a book. *Can you imagine having so many friends they wouldn't all fit in the house at once?* thought David.

He had a birthday coming up, and he was not above begging to attend.

"Please, Mom, please. Please, Dad, please."

Twenty or thirty pleases later, his parents agreed. Everything in Otters Holt was better than David remembered. The Christmas lights had all been replaced with purple and orange blinking strings that lit Main Street. Pumpkins and hay wagon displays were on every green space leading to Vilmer's Barn. Barbecue vendors lined the streets, tickling his tummy.

His mother was happier than he'd seen her in a long time. She hummed along to the fiddle music, smiling, even while his dad complained about parking.

David had his nose pressed to his half-lowered window; he had to elbow off the smudges every block. When the car finally stopped at the elementary school lot, Big T and David's cousin, Mash, were on a small dirt field, playing Wiffle ball with other kids his age. His grandfather towered over a little boy in a Batman costume, showing him how to hold a bat.

"Mom, can I?" David asked.

In the front seat, Hattie exchanged a look with John. John lowered his chin and said, "You stay with Tyson. Do you hear me?"

David was out the door at a sprint.

Big T stopped helping Batman to throw David, whom he called Buckaroo, into the air, and then he added him to the game. Buckaroo didn't need his grandfather to show him how to hold the bat. He smashed the ball to the edge of the dirt, making all the boys *whoop* and *hoot*. One little girl on the bleachers clapped for him as he crossed home plate.

Later, when the game was tied, it was Batman's turn to hit.

Big T called out, "Take off that mask and you'll be better."

Exasperated, Batman removed the mask and laid it carefully next to the little girl on the bleachers.

David's jaw dropped. "You're a girl," he said to Batman.

"Yeah, so?" she said. She strutted back to home plate and sent a pitch sailing into the grass—the farthest hit of the day.

He slapped her a high five as she crossed home plate. "I didn't know Batman could be a girl."

She huffed. "Well, Buckaroo, a girl can be anything."

David stored that memory in his secret heart. His mother had told him he'd been born with a second heart, and he could keep any secret he wanted in there.

The secrets that day sounded like this: *I wish I lived at Big T's house. I wish my mom were happier. I wish I could be like Batman.*

Third-grade math trouble became fourth-grade football trophies became fifth-grade growth spurts became sixth-grade acne became seventh-grade first kisses. By the time David was a teenager, he'd forgotten about his secret heart, but he hadn't forgotten that wearing a costume meant you could be anyone you wanted.

PART THREE

THE RAGING SUCCESS OF FAILURE

*Basically we're all looking for someone who knows who
we are and will break it to us gently.*
—ROBERT BRAULT

27

Eight. That's how many moves we made before I entered first grade. That may not sound too traumatic for a six-year-old. Six-year-olds aren't even responsible for packing their own toys. But I was a million years old at six, and I noticed. I remember the fear Mom lived with. How she stopped unpacking her paints so she didn't have to pack them back up again. She seemed uncertain that this was the life for her. Uncertain that they'd brought me into the middle of something so tumultuous. Meanwhile, Dad bumped us from town to town, proselytizing his way to larger congregations, soulfully preaching his way home to Community Church. The church where his own faith journey began. He was baptized at that altar. I was dedicated and confirmed at that altar. Fair or not, I understand why he's asking my emotions to take a backseat.

I zombie over to the worktable. My cell is ablaze with messages from Janie Lee and one from Woods. Hers are still coming in.

Woods: *You okay, McCaffrey?*

Janie Lee: *Shit. Shit. Shit.*

Janie Lee: *Does he hate us?*

Janie Lee: *Will he tell?*

Janie Lee: *Will Tawny?*

Janie Lee: *When you get this, will you please text me back?*

Janie Lee: *I'm really sorry.*

I send her a heart text, the old fashioned <3, not the big red annoying emoji heart. At the moment, that's all I manage. It stops the flow of her questions.

I text Woods instead.

Billie: *I need you.*

Woods: *On my way.*

Billie: *Cut your headlights. Park on the road.*

Woods: *Which door?*

Billie: *Garage.*

Between texting him and Woods's arrival, I arrange all the materials I've collected for Beauty and the Beast costumes. Turns out, the service projects for senior citizens were a real gold mine for LaserCon. Starburst wrappers, yellowed book pages, blue buttons, fur from Mr. Nix's coat, fifteen pairs of fur-lined slippers (not unlike the ones worn by my dad) that can be cut, sewn, and inverted, the hundreds of newspapers I've collected for the Daily Sit. It's not everything, but it's a very good start.

My hands need this task to drop my heartrate. My heart needs Woods.

I'm going to tell him everything, and he's going to fix this. Woods arrives, stealthily.

"I thought we'd work while we talk," I say, because I am not ready yet.

"'Kay, what are we building this evening?"

"Costumes. Beauty and the Beast, Billie-style. Sorry it's so late," I apologize unnecessarily.

"Oh, I was up. Had to drop off some *Save the Harvest Festival* signs at Abram's house. He always goes bowling with Martha on Friday nights." That's all Woods says about that. As if everyone else his age has spent their night in the same fashion. "Tell me what to do."

I hold up the newspapers. "We make their outfits from papier-mâché. Belle's dress and the trim on Beast's jacket come from those"—I show him the yellowed book pages I've removed from their bindings—"and supplement with these." He sees the bags of Starburst I've raided from every grocery and gas station in town.

"All right."

"These blue buttons from Lois Carter's basement can trim Beast's coat."

"Yep," he says, nodding his approval.

"We'll Photoshop a red rose to blue, and use those to cover the majority of Beast's coat." A computer and printer are set up opposite Guinevere for projects of this nature.

He likes the symbolism of roses. "Good, yes, love it," he says. "Billie, what are we actually building here?"

A piece of chicken wire eats into my palm and I cuss. I wipe my hands on my jeans and grab a Band-Aid from the shelf. Woods takes the wrapper from me and peels apart the Band-Aid. Gently, he attaches the adhesive around the broken skin.

And then I start at the beginning, and leave nothing out.

He listens, brain whirling. Our technology teacher, Mr. Winnows, showed us a video once of the first computers: heavy, loud, blinking, room-sized machines. That is Woods as he puts his head in the crease of his arms. When he raises his head, flips his cap from front to back, he has a plan.

"This is what we're going to do. I'm going to text the Hexagon. They're going to come over and we're going to build these costumes with you. Then, next weekend, you and Davey will win a thousand dollars and give it to the Save the Harvest Festival fund during KickFall. And then we're going to raise two thousand dollars with KickFall tickets. That'll be three thousand dollars, which you are going to hand the mayor as a donation. That should do it, Billie."

"What if they think I'm trying to buy the award?" I ask.

"You let me take care of that part."

"And Tawny?"

He hmms. "I'm not sure yet. But thank God she loves Janie Lee."

"And my dad?"

"Let's pray he understands."

"Woods, I wish I'd never been nominated. This would probably still matter, but it wouldn't matter as much."

His hand strokes his chin. "We'll fix this, B. You'll win the Corn Dolly. You won't have to move. I swear it."

"Woods?"

"Yes?"

"How come you aren't hurt by all this?"

"The same reason you aren't," he says simply. "We'd know if we were supposed to be together. I mean . . . haven't we known everything else when it comes to each other?"

I am so relieved he understands. That he is just as uncomplicated as he's always been.

He texts Mash, Fifty, and Davey, but not Janie Lee, just in case Dad returns to the garage. They arrive like sneaky ninjas. After a short speech that leaves out all the whys and explains the have-tos, he divides the tasks evenly among us.

Everyone nods. No questions asked.

"We are the Hexagon," Woods says.

Fifty laughs and says, "Uh, technically, we're a pentagram tonight."

No one touches that comment.

Time slips away, mostly in the cutting of roses. I use a mannequin I've named Jim. I shape clothing molds from chicken wire that I will eventually cut away. I measure Davey and he measures me. Our waists are the same but he has six inches of height on me.

Midnight. One a.m. Two a.m. Fifty and Davey have cut

seventy roses. Woods has ironed crinkles from the Starburst wrappers and stripped fur from the moccasins. Mash has run to the gas station and gotten us all caffeine and Twizzlers. I am drying layers of glue with a shop fan.

The radio is playing plucky music that keeps us annoyed, but awake.

I think about my father, who is on the other side of the garage door, probably thinking about me. I think about Janie Lee, who is on the other side of town, probably thinking about me. I think about Davey, who is on the other side of Guinevere, probably thinking about Waylan Academy. I think about Woods, who is beside me, assessing the molds. I think about Fifty and Mash, who dropped everything to be here. The garage is so full of thoughts I need to find somewhere else to put the tools.

A little after three, Davey tosses sixty, maybe seventy more roses on the desk and cusses a hand cramp. "This is starting to come together," he announces. "In fact, this might be the best costume I've ever been part of. We could win. Billie, we could win."

"Of course you will," says Woods, who knows less about LaserCon than I do.

And because Davey has won five straight years, and Woods is never wrong, I believe them.

28

Tawny is not at church the next day. "See you Sunday" was a lie. I am super relieved. So is Dad. He doesn't say it, but he shows a new couple with a baby to her regular seat, and that tells me he's thinking about her.

I use every boy in the Hexagon as a barricade between Janie Lee and me in the front pew. I do not speak to her or make eye contact, satisfying myself with only a single glance at her during the Lord's Prayer. My silent treatment is unfair, but I just . . . I look up at my father, in his robe and stole, living the single greatest dream in his life, and I need him to know I'm trying.

His eyes ricochet from her to me, and we both cower.

Mash punches me in the thigh when I nearly nod off. This has not been a weekend for sleep.

After lunch, we go door-to-door, selling KickFall tickets and spreading our Save the Harvest Festival message of joy. Me and Mash. Davey and Fifty—they, of course, argue over taking Fifty's Jeep or Davey's Camaro. We spend three hours driving every road in the county.

Landscaping is the only item left to do at the elementary school, so Woods and Janie Lee spend that time transplanting chrysanthemums, daylilies, and Japanese anemones from behind Mr. Nix's shed. When I asked Woods about the pairings, he said, "Mash and Davey are the grandsons of Tyson Vilmer. People need to see them." But I hadn't meant that. I meant, *Thank you for giving me space.*

We sell five hundred KickFall tickets and recruit nearly enough people for two teams of twenty. The committee might not think we can do this, but the town is voting otherwise.

At five o'clock, we straggle into Youth Suite 201, dirty and hopeful. I'm avoiding Janie Lee. She's avoiding me. She walks straight through the door and takes the farthest seat from the couch where I've thrown my tired body down.

"Let's talks about our glads, sads, and sorries," Dad begins.

And when it is my turn, I lie. And in doing so, I realize, we all lie, every week. This exercise is nearly pointless. No one wants their minister to know the real shit. Especially not when the minister is your dad and he already knows the realest of real shit.

He doesn't call me on the lie, but he looks so sad.

Scriptures are read. Prayers are said. The benediction is

given, and I have survived another encounter with the living church, Scott McCaffrey, and Janie Lee Miller. She leaves without a good-bye.

I am hurting her.

And I hate myself for it.

We should be pinging texts back and forth about how sorry we are or how awkward this is, but neither of us starts the conversation. I want to. What do I say? *I promised my father I wouldn't kiss you anymore.* That would just make things worse.

I slip from the youth room, down the steps, and into the sanctuary. The organ pipes are three stories tall, lining the back wall. The streetlights push through the stained glass, coloring the rose carpet a lighter shade of pink. The cavern-sized room is neither light nor dark, but something in between. So am I.

I sit rather than kneel at the altar. I fold myself into a ball, ashamed of the stockpiling emotions. On the cushion beneath me is an embroidered scene of David and his slingshot. Smooth polished wood I once held as Dad touched water to my forehead is at my back. There are splotches of wine on the carpet dripped from the crusts of bread during communion. All these things are a comfort. Years of tradition and faith.

I know what I want. I want to be able to look God in the face and say, "I did my best." I want to know that kissing Gerry or Janie Lee didn't change how He loves me. I want to be committed to Him and feel free to be myself. But I am terrified that I will always be trapped between my beliefs and my desires.

"What do I do?" I ask. The question lifts above the banners to the top of the organ pipes and through the ceiling.

Someone clears a throat on the other side of the altar. It's chesty, old, female. "You forgive yourself." From here, these words are a shadow behind the drum set and baby grand piano, but they are music.

Maybe God is in this room. And this voice is somehow his proxy. Whoever it is leaves before I take my head from between my knees. But I have heard the answer I came here for?

I pull out my phone and text Janie Lee. It's not much, but it's a starting place.

Billie: *I'm sorry I've been quiet.*

Three little dots appear on the screen, but whatever she's typing, she does not press Send.

Mom's minivan waits on the curb to drive me home from youth group. She asks no questions. We have our own *Save the Harvest Festival* sign posted at the end of our driveway and a bumper sticker as well. Woods. Always coming up with something new and better.

Mom deposits me in the garage and returns to her studio. We often retreat into cracks. But she shows up thirty minutes later and lands on the fridge. Her perfume wafts over the smell of epoxy. She sips her Diet Coke through a straw. My mother is dainty. Small-boned. Pixie-ish. She has steel-gray eyes and a hard-lined nose that's easy to draw because it's so damn straight. I look more like Dad in the face, but I have that same nose.

After several moments of silent sipping, she asks what I'm working on.

This question is taboo among the artists at our house. Her presence is nearly taboo as well. See, hear, and speak no evil. The spare bedroom is her studio. I don't go there; she doesn't come here. My choice. Art is subjective, and I've never been able to stomach her opinions. Every suggestion she makes, I take. Eventually, we realized that her chin over my shoulder meant I'd never create anything uniquely mine.

"Costumes," I tell her.

"You want some help?"

I raise my safety glasses. "Seriously?"

"Sure."

"Dad put you up to this?" I ask unfairly.

Dad rides everyone about something. The church members about holiness. Me about clothes, behavior, attitude. Mom about spending time with me. By his thinking, I'd be more like her—an improvement—if she spent more time and had more influence on me. He can't see that I'm already like her on the inside. His life exists in human exchanges, physical bartering. Mom and I, well, we exist in much more incorporeal space. I don't measure her love in hours spent with me. I measure it in hours spent understanding me.

"Oh, honey, Dad doesn't put me up to anything anymore. Tell me what I can do to help," she says.

Tell me I'm going to be okay.

The papier-mâché designs are in top form. Davey's

shoulders fit easily inside Beast's coat. I've installed zippers for Belle's dress, my dress. The top is an exact pattern of her yellow Disney outfit; the bottom ruffles to the floor. It remains to be seen whether it can be worn more than once. Papier-mâché is stiff. I imagine I'll be able to get it on but will be cutting it off.

The remaining work is tedious.

"All these have to be covered," I tell her. I've written what textile goes where on the papier-mâché. A color-by-number costume. Blue roses on Beast's coat. Yellow Starbursts up the lapel. Soft yellowed book pages over most of Belle's dress. The Hexagon got everything prepped, but I have the laborious task of sticking everything down and Mod Podging the hell out of it.

Mom strokes the fur pieces from Mr. Nix's coat and the slippers. I've sewn paws and claws that look relatively authentic. "Halloween?" she asks.

"LaserCon."

I had a pediatrician before we moved here, last name was something I couldn't pronounce. One night when I had a severe stomachache that Dad was positive presented as appendicitis, he bundled me in a blanket and tore off to the doctor's house. They laid me out on his kitchen counter, between the KitchenAid mixer and the toaster. The doctor ran his hands under warm water, and then pressed very gently around on my tummy, asking, *Elizabeth, does this hurt, sweetie?* Mom does something akin to that now. Presses gently. "You doing okay?" Press. "I see your brain working. You're struggling." Press.

"You can talk to me." Just like with that doctor, I am deeply aware that she does not intend to hurt me.

While we glue and cut and trim, the story is pieced together too. My feelings for Davey. Me kissing Janie Lee. Tawny and Dad seeing. Me being so damn confused. Surely Dad has already told her, so it doesn't matter what I say.

I feel emptied out.

She adds a Starburst line to Beast's coat. I ask a question. "Are you angry with me?"

The glue pauses midair. "Billie, I have a million emotions right now. Anger isn't one of them."

"Disappointment?"

"No, sweetie."

Her lack of judgment opens a door I assumed would be dead-bolted. "What do you think I should do?"

"In this case, your life is your art, and no one, *no one* but you can tell you how to finish this piece. You just have to live it and see how it turns out. And if you don't like it, you do what I do when I'm working on a canvas that goes south."

"What's that?"

"You paint over it," she says. Such a simple solution.

"Will the church really let me do that?"

"This has nothing to do with the church. God? Sure. Ask Him what He wants if that's something you wish to do. But He and the church are not necessarily the same on this."

We work alongside each other for several more hours. I haven't said much since I said everything. We're okay with the silence, semi-okay. "You really don't care who I date?" I ask.

"I care that you find someone kind and loving. Someone who won't let you hide. Someone who pushes you to be a better person. But there is nothing I've seen in Janie Lee or Davey that worries me."

"But Dad said—"

"You're not talking to Dad. Baby, I went to art school. I have many friends who have chosen many different lifestyles. They just don't live here."

I hadn't thought of it that way. I argue, "You married a preacher. Do you really think it doesn't bother him?"

"I married a preacher, not a saint," she says. "My faith in God is useless without trust. Maybe that's naïve, but I believe things will work out. With this costume. With Davey. With Janie Lee. With the Corn Dolly and the Harvest Festival. Even with your father and the church and the fire. All you have to do is be yourself."

"I don't know how to do that anymore."

"Sure you do. You've always known yourself really well. But someone's made you doubt that. I want my kid back. The one who set the church on fire."

I stop gluing. "You yelled at me about that."

She tsks. "It's a metaphor. You do you, sweetie. The rest will take care of itself."

By midnight, the costumes are finished, and I can feel my fire coming back.

29

Today is the first day of LaserCon: the day we win a thousand dollars.

We rendezvous at Molly the Corn Dolly at seven a.m. Then we pile into Woods's mom's Suburban.

In every other yard we pass, there is a promotional sign for the Harvest Festival. Woods has outdone himself. I've stolen him for moral support. I've stolen them all. Woods and Fifty in the front. Janie Lee and Mash in the middle. Davey and me in the back. Belle and Beast in the cargo hold.

When we decided to skip school as a group, Woods had Doc Robbins write Janie Lee an excuse.

"But what about you all?" she asks, accepting a powdered doughnut from Mash.

"Hell." Fifty giggles, steals the doughnut from her hand.

"We can't all have heavy menstrual problems."

"It does not say that." She unfolds the doctor's note, reads for herself, and crams it into a pocket of her backpack.

Woods is turning onto the interstate, admitting he suffered from an unfortunate loss of imagination when he spoke with Doc Robbins last night. Janie Lee is as red as a channel bass, and we're all ripping with laughter. Sounds about right to me. Sounds much better than the awkwardness of this past week.

I am not worried about my excuse to Otters Holt High School. One for Dad? Well . . . that could be a problem. He can always be a problem. Especially right now, when he is eagle-eyeing my life for signs of Janie Lee. I could have told Mom, should have after she helped me with the costumes, but no one else told their mom. Which meant I stole a piece of bacon from the plate this morning and said I'd see her later. She'd told me she was excited about KickFall tomorrow, and I'd said, "Me too." All truths.

Pastureland becomes fast food exits become Nashville. The Music City Center wows from the interstate. The wavy roof sits low on the skyline, well beneath the Batman building, just as imposing. It is two, no, three blocks wide. Woods exits.

I am unprepared for the overflow of LaserCon attendees. Inhabitants of Middle-earth, post-apocalyptic Georgia, Asgard, and many more crowd the sidewalk. Three stormtroopers and a herd of guys and girls dressed as characters from *300* draw the attention of every vehicle on the road.

They are all a thing of beauty. A world apart from Otters Holt and Nashville.

"Crazy-ass people," Fifty mutters.

"What a wonderment," Woods says.

"These are my people," Davey comments quietly.

Janie Lee steals a glance in my direction. I wink. She winks back. All week long we have been attempting normalcy. Not postkiss us. Not kiss us. The us that has existed from the moment I hauled her ass out of Kentucky Lake. It's been a bit like climbing Everest, but the dual winks are a good sign we're coming back.

Police barricades block the front of the convention center. "I think, children, I'll have to drop you off and park," Woods announces. "Can I trust you not to get into too much trouble?"

Horns blare, urging him to pull away from the curb. Everyone hops out. I shoulder two duffel bags of accessories and Davey balances Belle and Beast on the sidewalk. "Text us," I say to Woods.

He's already pulling away from the curb, driving as if he knows where he's going when he most certainly does not.

Gerry and Thom's last text swears they are heading our way. This convergence excites me. We are in a hive of super-heroes. People who must meet here every year are hugging and dueling and drinking and striking poses. Three *Dragon Ball Z* friends chat about attending a manga session. A gang of Marvel characters talking up Stan Lee, who is rumored to be attending. Every third or fourth person is a Potterhead. There are no ages, no genders. Bodies are hidden completely, or totally exploited. That's the peculiar thing that happens when you pretend to be someone else: you are someone else.

I get to be *Elizabeth McCaffrey, born 1999—d. ? R.I.P.: Princess.* Who the hell saw that coming? But I think I can do it. And it will not be like Billie Wears a Dress to School Day. I'm doing this because I want to. Not because I feel obligated. And I made this costume myself.

A deep, booming voice calls out, "Hey, McCaffrey, who you gonna call?" The yelling Ghostbuster is Thom. Gerry's dressed as Lara Croft, and damn. She's dyed her green hair as black as Janie Lee's. I make the introductions.

Davey is easy today. Relaxed. He has none of the pensive energy from the time when we didn't know how to navigate each other. We are in his playground, and he is confident.

Thom puts Beast under his arm, chides me with mock-worry. "I'm not sure you've done enough work on these."

We all laugh. I want to thank Thom for saying this. For making Davey smile so broadly.

There's so much concrete. So much gray. Even though I am happy to be among the mill of humanity, I can't imagine living here in all this noise. Davey will probably live here again soon, and I'll return to the trees and the majesty of Kentucky Lake. I hope.

"You okay?" Davey asks.

"Yes," I say. "I'm excited."

"Belle and Beast are amazing," he says for the millionth time.

We follow Thom, juggling the duffel bags while Thom calls over his shoulder for Davey to come along and be useless *inside* the convention center. Woods knocks into me—he's just joined us without needing a text—and says, "I like him." So I say, "Who doesn't?" Because it's true. With their combined forces, Thom and Woods could take over a small country by lunch.

We check in and register for the costume contest. Fairly simple rules of engagement. Davey and I are assigned a photo booth time when we will strike a pose. The photo will be judged. Fifty candidates will be chosen to appear in the ballroom. Showdown at high noon. Our assigned photo booth time is 10:45. Twenty-five minutes from now. There is no time to waste.

We get cracking, taking over a family bathroom on the second floor to assemble our twosome. Gerry tells me, "You're gonna be so effing hot in this. You're like one of those exploding stars." I like to watch Woods watching her, analyzing how she became the creature she is. Janie Lee nudges his arm so he'll stop staring, and Gerry tells them both that she is taking my boots while I'm wearing Mom's terrible yellow high heels. And then she says, "Shall I kiss them, Billie?"

"It *is* your standard greeting," I say, knowing she is trolling the boys.

Fifty says, "Well, I'd like that."

It was a very Fifty thing to say until Mash says, "Uh, yeah, me too," as quiet as a confession. Thom gives Mash a little fist bump.

Davey catches my eye in the mirror. He's pleased our friends are getting along so smashingly. He's excited about LaserCon. He says, "When you said you'd help, I had no idea you'd pull this off. I should have. I mean . . . you're you."

"Don't thank me yet. We've only got one shot at putting them on," I say.

After some maneuvering and strategizing, Thom picks Davey up at the waist and sets him neatly inside the Beast's pants. Fifty does this for me, telling me I am never allowed to make papier-mâché clothes again and to eat more lettuce.

Janie Lee and Gerry help me into the top of Belle's dress. Gerry handles my zipper, her cold fingers raking up my back. I give Davey the fur pieces for his legs, face, and arms, envying that he will be warm. Makeup time.

My face becomes the property of Janie Lee. She is nearly as close as she was when we kissed. I close my eyes so I am not tempted to make this moment more than it is. Davey turns his face over to Gerry. When they finish, we have three minutes to get to the photo booth.

We hurry on papier-mâchéd legs, take a regal picture, and then set about the arduous task of waiting. Thom and Gerry are off like the cat and mouse of their namesakes, seeing panels they do not have tickets to and promising to meet us later. Fifty, Mash, Woods, and Janie Lee leave us in search of pancakes. Davey and I remain standing near the ballroom because the flaw in this design is that there's no sitting of any kind.

"What do you usually do with the money?" I ask Davey.

"What money?"

"The winnings?"

"Oh, I put it in savings. Dad always insists. Nice to think we'll give it away this time, though."

"Did you make a decision about Waylan?"

"Yep," he says. "I'm staying in Otters Holt."

I ask what changed his mind and if he has told his dad.

After a pause, he begins. "The other night in your garage. We were all working on the costumes, and the clock was ticking, and I was thinking, I'm really happy here." He gives a full smile. "You're a part of that, you know?"

"I like being part of that," I say.

"It's pretty cool that we've come full circle."

"What do you mean?"

"We met when we were kids. It was at a Harvest Festival. Maybe 2007 or 2008. You were playing Wiffle ball with Big T in a Batman mask."

I have a vague memory of Wiffle ball. And an even vaguer one of Batman. I'd gone around for a week or so in a costume. "At the elementary school?" I ask.

"Yep. And I hate to tell you this, but superheroes suck at Wiffle ball."

I want to punch him, but if I do, I would put a hole in Beast's jacket.

His fingers are slim and busy, drumming the wall as he continues. "I assumed you were a boy until you took your mask off. And then you said something about being able to be anything you wanted. I can't remember the exact words, but it left an impression."

I don't remember him. I remember hitting a home run. Memories are lopsided sometimes.

"That's what started me on costumes," he says. "You. Batman. It was like I found a piece of myself in Otters Holt then, and another piece of myself there this fall. Waylan is fine. Thom and Gerry are . . . well, they're Thom and Gerry, we won't change no matter where we live."

"Your relationship amazes me. You move so easily around feelings."

He laughs a raucous laugh. "Not always," he says.

He tells me their story. A story that changes and rearranges the pieces.

How freshman year, some guys at Waylan started calling Thom and him the Oxford Homos, among other titles. So when Woods put me on the guys' side of the Hexagon, he didn't have to imagine my confusion; he'd felt it. He spent hours dissecting what made his peers, even some faculty at Waylan, ship them. They both had girlfriends when it started. They never experimented with clothes or makeup, apart from LaserCon. As far as he could tell, they existed outside stereotypes.

"Maybe it's because we never shied away from physical contact. Thom's dad is a counselor, his mom a kindergarten teacher; he was raised on a diet of hugs and kisses," he says, and then goes on to tell me that he has never been naturally touchy-feely. That Thom was his only friend for so long that he grew to enjoy his brotherly affection. "He has a way of disarming everyone."

I nod at that.

"Looking back, I think people were jealous. Thom was just coming into his charisma, and everyone else was years away from having a personality. He could have lavished his affection on them, but he'd chosen me and they hated me for it."

To shut up the barrage of voices, Thom, who has since decided he is demisexual, kissed him. No asks. No buildup. They were playing video games one minute, kissing the next. That could not have been easy to do at thirteen. Even for Thom.

"After that when someone yelled, 'Hey homos,' I heard them, but I knew I wasn't gay. I'd . . . well, I'd given it my best go, and I still liked girls. He liked girls too. And boys. And anyone who made him feel deeply. Which I did. So I get why he kissed me. And he gets why I didn't want us to be *that* to each other. Most people want puddles to splash around in; Thom wants souls where scuba diving is encouraged."

That was about the best description I'd heard of Thom. And it made sense why he fit so well with Gerry. They are creatures of equal depth for different reasons. If I knew Gerry for a thousand years, she would tell me a story about herself I'd never heard before.

"You thought we were together," he says. "That's why you asked me if I was jealous of Gerry?"

"I . . . yeah," I admit. "I was trying to get you to tell me in the car."

"And I was trying to not confuse you. You'd kissed Woods. You were considering Janie Lee. I thought throwing myself in the mix was douche and insensitive."

"So you let me believe you were gay?"

"I only tried to let you believe that I love Thom. And I do."

That makes sense. I still wish I'd known. It would have made my attraction to him not feel so ridiculous.

He explains that after their experimenting he stopped caring about everyone else's opinions and listened when Thom assured him, "They're shallow, bro," and "We know who we are."

"Billie, this shit is murky and personal. You had to be able to explore," he says as a conclusion.

I tell myself he has a special Billie Edition Telescope that allows him this view. He is sure Janie Lee will be fine, whatever we decide. He is also sure we will win a thousand dollars.

"I mean, look at us," he says.

Look at us, I think.

Our cell phones buzz with news. We've made the Laser-Con costume cut.

We kill the next half hour making up things we'd do

with a thousand dollars if we weren't giving it to the Harvest Festival. Buy seeds for Mr. Nix? Get Thom some better rims? Purchase Gerry a shitty car so she doesn't have to ride the bus to Denny's when Thom's at school? Dozens of footballs for the Spandex Junkwagons? Canvases for Mom? A new concordance for Dad? (He'd personally like a complete set of expensive dictionaries.) A couch more comfortable than the Daily Sit?

Davey offers another spontaneous option. "We could give it to the church. For the fire damages."

"That would be nice," I say. I'd love for my dad to know that even though I look different than him on the outside, we have similar insides.

"Assuming we win."

"Don't go doubting us now," I say. "I like assuming we'll win."

One hour later, we have walked, paraded, posed, twirled, been examined and celebrated by a ballroom full of attendees and judges. This is a competition for nerds. Bonus points for special effects.

Fifty contestants are cut to ten. Ten are cut to two. Gerry and Thom and the Hexagon cheer as we make progress. Our remaining competition stands on stilts, towering over us, and is covered in actual bark from top to bottom. I'm not sure which character he intends to be—I am woefully bad at fandom—but his height alone is extraordinary. We've been lamenting our inability to bend and stretch; this dude has to balance.

Regardless, we have made it this far, and I am ready to

collect my money and save Molly the Corn Dolly from being a cliché.

"Ladies and gentlemen," an announcer says. "The judges of the 2017 LaserCon Costume Contest have selected a winner. It is my pleasure to award this check of *one thousand dollars*"—he reveals a big cardboard check from behind the podium—"to . . ."

The announcer then transforms into a masochistic bastard who allows the audience to pant with anticipation. My heart is on fire.

"A tale as old as time! David Winters and Elizabeth McCaffrey in their reimagining of Beauty and the Beast," he yells into the microphone.

In the front aisle, Woods waves his arms like a conductor.

Fifty screams, "We're walking the beam, bitches."

Janie Lee blows me a kiss.

30

I like winning. I even like winning in a dress. I like winning next to Davey. I like Janie Lee's fingers pressed against her mouth and then sending me love across the room.

I like it so much it spills into every fiber, every cell. I twirl. Everyone should feel like this. Even Tawny Jacobs. Ten years of losing can't be easy when this is what winning feels like.

Back in the family bathroom, Davey and I are cutting ourselves free from Belle and Beast. We're alone with our cardboard check and costume deconstruction. The others are getting food. Again.

Davey is leaning close to the mirror, removing signs of Beast, applying signs of Davey. He traces dark lines around his lids, and I review what I know about him. Dorky. Passionate. Helpful. He likes good music; doesn't care if it's popular.

School isn't hard for him. Making friends is. There's no such thing as casual contact. He loves his complicated dick of a dad. Loves his best friend. Shares some of the same questions about sexuality and faith as me, despite having grown up in a different household.

He's a bright, bright soul.

"You're thinking hard over there," he says to me.

I sigh at being caught. And then my stomach growls—low and rattling like an animal—because we, unlike the crew, haven't stopped to eat all day. He pokes me in the stomach, and I poke him back, and then we are grappling, laughing, giddy that we have won.

Then, the six inches of height between the top of his head and the top of mine no longer exist. His lips are inches from mine, paused, asking politely, but longing to kiss me.

"I still don't want to confuse you," he says.

The slightest pressure of his body against mine is heavy. And warm. We're both sweating from the costumes and smelling like powder from the makeup. Buzzing, delirious. The day is a Russian doll, unnesting layers I did not know existed.

I say, "Maybe it'll help," because I cannot imagine letting this moment pass.

We both turn our heads, and then our lips are on each other, hungry. I kiss him too hard, too aggressively. As if I have something to prove. There is pride in our tongues from a day spent winning what we want. He matches me stride for stride, and I don't think he minds that I use my teeth. No one else could have kissed me like that. Not even Gerry, who is freer than anyone I know. This isn't freedom; this is release. I let myself feel everything, the way I haven't with everyone else because I've been too busy thinking to feel.

And at the end of it, I am a dandelion, and Davey is a gale-force wind. He scatters me everywhere. Part of me lands back in Kentucky, caught in Molly the Corn Dolly's large hand. Another bit of fluff drifts to Missouri and lands atop the arch in Saint Louis. Another crosses the Mississippi River into Illinois.

Our foreheads are still glued together, both of us catching our breath, when Mash says, "Uh, guys, Woods is out front with the Suburban," and I think, *Damn, one of these days I'm going to kiss someone and no one will interrupt it.*

"You okay?" he asks when Mash closes the door.

"I'm . . ." What am I? "I'm not sorry."

"Good."

"You're not gay," I say, because it keeps occurring to me.

He grins. "Nope. But you've got a lot going on, and if you'd rather be with her, I won't make it hard for you."

The best thing about Davey in this moment: he doesn't expect me to say anything else. We pack the rest of our stuff and reemerge as if nothing has happened.

We are annoying as hell on the way home. We honk the horn, which sounds like a dying mule. Twice, Woods pulls the Suburban over, and we run laps around it like hooligans. When he reaches town and drives into Molly's parking lot, he makes us take a picture saluting her. We are idiotic, happy. I'd like to drive too fast or run through a cornfield with my arms in the air. I am alive and weightless.

"We should bottle this," I scream.

"No," Woods says. "I've got a better idea."

"We should share it," we say together.

"You two are fucking annoying," Fifty says, pushing at Woods's head and rolling his eyes. "We're gonna have to do some new project, aren't we?"

"Yeah, you are. And I know just the one," I say.

And there we are, back in my garage, everyone pressed around tables, tearing pages from old, destroyed books, like I did for Belle. Mash straddles the chair backward and whispers, "I gotta get a girlfriend so I stop getting drafted for this shit." I tell him we'd just draft her too, so he should get right on that.

He pops a Dorito into his mouth, smiles like he knows who he has in mind, and starts folding papers according to my example. "You ever think you maybe have an oral fixation?" I ask. He must have the metabolism of a hummingbird.

His lips search for the straw and he whispers, "You ever think you're fixated on my cousin?"

I deserved that.

I lean in to Mash's ear. "Did you know he was straight all along?"

Close to us, everyone is folding paper. We could so easily be overheard, but he is careful, angling his mouth where no one will read his lips. "Are you straight, B?"

"I'm complicated," I answer.

"Yep," Mash says, his shoulders already falling before they ever got totally into the shrug. "Guess I knew that already."

"Secrets. Secrets," Woods calls, not wanting to be left out.

Mash handles that straightaway. "I was asking if she had more chips in the house."

Here's a thing about Mash. He's everyone's secret keeper. When he does choose a girlfriend, he'll have her for the rest of his life.

Here's a thing about Fifty. He always asks the obvious question. "So are there?"

"Are there what?" I ask, dumbly.

"More chips, asshole," he says, scoffing.

"I'll go see."

"I'll come with you," Janie Lee says.

This is the first time she is voluntarily placing herself near me in front of my parents. We have to start somewhere. Mom and Dad are watching/not-watching TV in the living room. Janie Lee flips them a strange wave, and I announce that we're getting chips.

"What are you all up to out there?" Dad inquires, and Janie Lee blushes.

"Hexagon things," I say.

Dad, who is in a jovial mood, snuggles closer to Mom and says, "Please do not burn the garage down."

"There are two things for sure in this world. One, I'll die in these boots, and two, I will never hurt the garage."

"There's my girl," Mom says.

"Your girl," Dad repeats. "Yep. But she's my girl tomorrow for KickFall."

I am her girl when I'm burning things. His girl when I'm winning. At least they're excited about the game. No amount of excitement keeps him from watching Janie Lee and me too closely, suspiciously.

All we have are those colored veggie-stick things that taste like air. Mash won't care, but everyone else will. "Popcorn?" Janie Lee asks, and I agree. We wait on the microwave to ding. As the kernels heat and pop, she says, "Was I weird just then?"

"Yeah, but it's okay."

"We're okay?" she asks.

The microwave dings. "I am if you are," I say. And then, I don't know why, I say, "I kissed Davey. I'm telling you because I didn't want to lie about it."

She backs toward the dishwasher, grips the counter behind her. I am studying her expression, and she says, "Are you saying I lied about something?"

"No. I just want to level. Because we're us."

"Oh. Okay." The *oh* is painfully spoken; the *okay* shows some recovery. "Thank you. I'll be glad to be us again."

I wonder which us she means.

She takes the veggie sticks, and I snag the popcorn, and we gift the Hexagon with these spoils. Fifty's napping on one end of the Daily Sit. He snarls only a little, either at waking up or my lack of flavorful provisions. He goes back to sleep and the rest of us fold and tape for hours.

I did the right thing in telling her, but that shocked look plays in a loop. When I walk her to the car, she asks to play her violin to me over the phone when she gets home. That tells me her state of mind: keyed up. The Lindsey Stirling piece she plays is flawless. That tells me the state of her heart: aching.

When she picks the phone back up, and thanks me, she says, "Billie, you looked beautiful this morning as Belle. Thank you for inviting me to the Con."

I tell her I'll meet her the next morning at the elementary school, and she says good night. I don't think either of us sleeps.

31

There are so many cars in the elementary school parking lot we have to park them in the outfield. Woods has dressed Fifty in an orange vest and handed him a flag to direct traffic. Everyone in walking distance leaves cars at home. People line the sides of streets because the town doesn't have sidewalks except in front of the school. Mothers hold small sticky fingers and tote Cheerios and sippy cups. Fathers hoist toddlers up to rest on their shoulders and bump strollers along the road.

The weather is gorgeous. There's wind coming in off the lake so crisp and strong you can practically smell the fish being caught and cleaned. Mash cut the grass one last time this morning, and the smell of alfalfa clippings rises to my nostrils, tempting me to believe it's spring instead of fall. Everything is fresh and vivid. We sold eight hundred tickets in advance.

Woods swears we'll get two hundred more at the gate. Maybe three hundred.

My family lives nearly half a mile away, but the three of us walk over.

Mom whistles. "A great turnout, baby."

"Your mural is amazing," I say. She has spent the last week making her own special addition to the elementary school brick wall. Sixty-five years of Harvest Festivals are represented in various ways. The scene is amazing. Norman Rockwell meets Shepard Fairey. I would like to examine all the small details, but as we near the field, Janie Lee begins to play the national anthem on her violin, reminding me we are a little late to the pregame festivities. I pivot toward the flagpole, hand over my heart until the last note.

The kickball teams are divided up, each side wearing cheap mesh pullovers from the middle school gym. The teams are multigenerational. Woods made sure of it. The youngest member is the mayor's grandson, Caleb, who is seven and a real ballbuster. He's turning cartwheels by home plate. The oldest is Ada May Adcock. No less than four sports bras attempt to contain her abundant chest. Heaven help us, and her back, if she *runs* the bases. No cartwheels for her. Normally, Mash and I would play, but Woods says we shouldn't.

Mash being Tyson's hometown grandson, me being the Corn Dolly nominee.

"Oh, dear Lord," Mom says about Ada May, and we both laugh.

"Be kind," Dad reminds us.

The waistband of Janie Lee's short shorts is flipped over and she's wearing tall multicolored socks with purple otters on them. If this were olden times—two weeks ago—I would walk up and tell her she has an ass cheek hanging out. But now, I don't know. Can I still do that when we are what we are?

"Are you going to wish her luck?" Mom asks.

I say, "Yes," and start her way, wondering where my dad is and if he's watching. This was Dad and me this morning:

Him: "Tawny will be there."

Me: "I know."

He didn't have to say anything else.

I don't make it all the way to Janie Lee because Mash yells my name out the driver's window of his truck. He beats the door, whooping with excitement. "Make way for the man in the truck," Woods says to several families in the truck's path. Mash drives past Fifty's directional flag and parks between Mrs. Johnson's electric fence and the bleachers. He's out, using the tire as a step, and hopping into the bed before I can jog over and lend a hand. He hefts a Radio Flyer wagon into my arms.

I yawn. He yawns back and then stuffs some Big League Chew into his cheek. We toss the trash bags filled with last night's crafting spoils into the wagon.

"How do you want to do this?" he asks.

"They go to everyone," I tell him.

"Even the dudes?"

We made two thousand Book Dollies. I'm not taking them home.

"Even the dudes," I say.

He likes this idea, and says, "You know Big T's smiling right now."

Gerry and Thom, who have driven in for the day, offer to help, but we put them in jerseys and send them to separate teams. Mash and I set about the crowd, doling out Book Dollies—folded and tucked pieces of torn classics that were headed for the dump. Small origami gifts patterned after Molly.

I know basically how they will be received because at six a.m., Mom descended the steps into the garage in search of the newspaper. Mash had fallen asleep on the floor, and I had taken the couch. Everyone else had gone home around one. We were drowning in Dollies.

If Mom were a crier, she would have cried. She's not, so she smiled instead.

"I am not going soft," I said wearily, and put my head back down for five more minutes of sleep.

"I didn't say you were," she said.

Now, as I press Book Dollies into the hands of men and women alike, I think: maybe I am going a little soft. And maybe that's exactly the way I'm supposed to be.

With only one winner every year, the odds of earning a Dolly aren't high. I picture all the women like me—the ones who will never win—putting their Book Dolly in a special place when they get home. The mantel. The curio cabinet.

Maybe a hope chest. There is more than one way to add color to the world. More than one way to crown a queen.

I develop a little rhythm with greeting people. "In case it's the last Harvest Festival, everyone should get something to remember it by."

This works well and good until I get to the Spandex Junk-wagons. They've seen me gifting hundreds of dollies at this point. I can't conceivably skip them, and Mash is clear on the other side of the field, so there's no delegating.

The game is raging like the Super Bowl. Tied seven-seven. Davey has just kicked a home run. His second in three innings. I'd like to celebrate him. But no. I'm offering Margaret Lesley a Book Dolly and repeating my mantra.

She brings herself to give me a proper thank-you.

I've heaped some sugar on her sourness. That's satisfying in its own way.

Mash and I have only a limited number of Dollies left by the time we reach the front row. Mr. Nix sits there, Otis in his lap, and Kevin the home health aide by his side. He's eating a Little Debbie cake as if it is the only pleasure in the world. To his right, Grandy and Tawny Jacobs are talking fencerows. "The painting rates these days are ungodly." "I had three posts reset and it cost one hundred and fifty dollars. Can you believe it?" "I can."

One could not call this a friendly conversation because it is not happening between friends, but one could call it congenial.

This seating placement rings of Woods. Their bony tushes

are atop two UK bleacher chair backs owned by the Carringtons. I get his attention.

"Einstein rules the world," he yells back to me, because KickFall is doing more than raising money.

Janie Lee is beside him. One of her otter socks has fallen to her ankle. She's leaning over, tugging it back to her knee. I have a memory of the tall tube socks she wore in elementary school. No one at her house did much more than make sure she had boxed macaroni and cheese for dinner back then, so she always came to school dressed pell-mell. Tube socks as knee socks. Extra-large men's T-shirts as dresses. Knowing someone from first grade on, watching them turn from that to this, well, it's a piece of life art.

Hands empty, I walk to the backstop and wave her over. She laces her fingers through fencing. I lace mine on top of hers, intending to say, *Sorry I was late this morning*, but she jerks back as if I've slapped her.

"Not here," she whispers, eyes drifting toward Tawny. "Your dad."

I back away, embarrassed, and busy myself taking the wagon to Mash's truck. Will it always be this way? Will we always care about what everyone thinks?

Not long ago we swore that nothing would ever change us. Was that naïve? Can you put everything on the line and have it change nothing? Maybe. Woods and I are the same. Maybe even better. Easier. Because now every touch and look that passes between us isn't going somewhere. I don't hold my breath and wonder about our future. I just live. I want to be in that space with Janie Lee whether we are together or apart.

I wiggle into a seat beside Mr. Nix, praying he changes the sudden sullenness of my mood. Mr. Nix giddily cheers for Davey, who laps up the praise like gravy. Every trip to the plate, he phantom high-fives Mr. Nix. "Gloria would like our boy all grown up," he tells Kevin. Kevin doesn't correct Mr. Nix, and I'm glad for it.

Flowers line the kickball field. Transplanted mums trim the freshly painted playground. All from Mr. Nix. A group of kiddos are on the merry-go-round where I used to make myself dizzy; they're using a bag of leftover potting soil to drive Matchbox cars through. In the spring, the tulip bulbs will bloom, and I will bring Mr. Nix here and show him Gloria's garden. Her legacy of seeds and bulbs. The color *she* has added to the world.

"How are you liking my coat?" Mr. Nix asks. He remembers the coat but has forgotten Davey's name. With a wink and a grin, I tell him, "That coat is worth one thousand dollars."

Mr. Nix says, "A thousand-dollar coat for a thousand-dollar girl."

I'm drenched from running around with Mash. My hair's in a million hairpins. The bags under my eyes should be labeled cargo. The town got my makeover. I wouldn't change that. Women press Book Dollies against hearts and make them dance for gleeful daughters. They tell one another, "This is so nice," and point at Mash and me because we made the deliveries. Men have Dollies peeking out of breast pockets. Davey has his threaded through his bandanna.

KickFall and Book Dollies have done CPR on the dying heart of my town. The mayor and Woods shake, and he announces to the crowd through a jankety karaoke speaker system, "Ladies and gentlemen, today's efforts raised two thousand two hundred and ten dollars toward saving the Harvest Festival! Bravo!"

"Go up there." Woods knocks me off balance with a hand on the small of my back. I see that he duplicated the large cardboard check Davey and I were given at LaserCon. When I cannot find it in myself to move up the stairs to the stage, he trots up to the mayor himself and whispers something.

The mayor cups his hand over the microphone and listens. Then he says, "Well, this young man tells me that one of the Corn Dolly nominees won a costume party this week, and she's donating all the proceeds to the fund. Come on up here, Billie McCaffrey."

No one cares that I am a hot mess today. I hand over the cardboard check. Taking the microphone from his hand, I say, "It wasn't just me. That crew over there did it with me. Go on, stand up, Hexagon."

And they do. And everyone claps just as loudly for them.

"Save the Harvest Festival!" Woods yells like a cheerleader.

And again, because Woods has spoken, everyone in the stands echoes, "Save the Harvest Festival!" The mayor reins in the crowd with final instructions. "Now, if you can all make your way inside and cast your ballots. Thank you for coming out."

The field evacuates. Woods nudges my shoulder. "You'll win," he says.

I want to believe him. But this is the one place my imagination cannot stretch. If the Corn Dolly could be bought, nearly all the winners would have been different.

Politely, eyebrows inching toward his cap, eyes bouncing between Janie Lee and Davey, he says, "You'd better decide which of those two you'll be dancing with."

Every year, the winner of the Corn Dolly dances the first dance of the harvest. For unmarried candidates, the town uses this dance to start wedding registries at the Mercantile on Main. For the happily hitched, it's a barometer of health. Occasionally, it is used to predict divorce. Though only rarely, and the women are sympathetic, unless it's the woman stepping out.

My heart suddenly thuds in my ears. I have not thought of who I would dance with.

But it will not matter, because I won't win. *We* have saved the festival, not *me*.

"I see you over there, McCaffrey." Woods rocks all the way up on his toes with nervous energy. "And here's the problem with what you're thinking. We can't always be right, so you'd better have a plan if you're wrong. Especially if the town is watching."

"I'll figure it out if I have to," I say, feeling very positive that

I've finally found the thing that Woods Carrington is wrong about.

"Well, either way, you realize we have to walk that damn beam now. You know Fifty's about to have a heyday and a half."

We trudge toward the group, where the weariness of several hard weeks of manual labor strikes Fifty first. He throws himself in the middle of the pitcher's mound and yells, "Two thousand two hundred and ten dollars! Hot damn!" Even though it's too late to matter, he lifts his head and checks for small children.

"You're insufferable, Fifty," Mash says, which only serves to make Fifty happier.

He taunts us, repeating the number in victory. "Guess what that means, bitches?"

Woods lies beside Fifty and then Mash and Davey do the same. They are laid out like spokes on a wheel, letting the sun punish them. Janie Lee and I fall between them. We are a heap of dirt and limbs. "Do we really have to?"

Woods says, "Indeed, we must, or the stakes lose their power."

Everyone sighs a great big sigh except Fifty, who says, "Hell yeah," with several more syllables than are required.

32

Vilmer's Barn has large cross-beam sliding doors, a high loft window, and a half-hexagon-shaped metal roof. Once upon a time it had a vibrant paint job, but the weather has worn the bright-red colors into a lovely gray-and-maroon smudge. It's well built, sturdy considering its age. There's a narrow rafter stretching from loft door to loft door, nearly thirty feet in the air: Vilmer's Beam.

Unfortunately for us, the barn isn't full of straw and hay as it was the last time we walked Vilmer's Beam. The Harvest Festival's tables, chairs, and vendor booths are stacked and stored in neat rows beneath the beam, and it would take too long to move everything. Everyone cusses. Gerry, who trails Thom, who trails Davey, suggests that we're all *off our nut*. I'm inclined to agree.

I am tugged backward by my sweatshirt. The rest of the group files wearily by, Fifty in the lead, leaving me with Davey. His arms are folded over his chest. He is dubious. "Why?" he asks.

I give a very Billie answer. "Because we said we would."

"Do you do everything you say you will?" he asks the way someone might ask, *And if Woods jumped off a cliff, would you jump too?*

A million comebacks are on my lips. "Yes" comes out first.

"I'm not worried about you." He nods toward Janie Lee. Then, in the same fortuneteller voice in which he'd said, *You'll burn down the church,* he comments, "This is a bad idea." But that doesn't change anything. We're still going to walk the beam. He knows it. I know it.

Despite my confidence, we all have reservations. Fifty's digging a rut with his foot the way baseball players do when they step into the batter's box. Mash is a new shade of puking green.

Gerry and Thom park themselves at a table to watch. Like a row of monkeys, Mash, Fifty, Janie Lee, Davey, and I follow Woods to the loft ladder. I'm between the two least experienced walkers—Janie Lee and Davey. No problem. Rung by rung, higher and higher, we climb.

We are almost to the top. I touch Janie Lee's ankle. She stops, and I climb the side of the ladder, hanging out over the barn. "Are you okay?"

"Why wouldn't I be?"

"Just checking," I say.

But she is not okay, and I don't know whether to call her on it and make a scene or let her push through. She nearly steps on my fingers to keep climbing. I swing back around and continue ascending the ladder. When I arrive at the top, I position myself under the eaves so Davey has room to join us. Thomas and Gerry are a million miles away. Our line begins inching across the beam like kindergartners walking to the playground, Woods at the lead. Everything on point.

"One foot in front of the other," Janie Lee says to no one in particular. Certainly not to me.

The looming beam stretches out yard on yard. Her fear is so palpable that no amount of internal chanting releases my anxiety that she will fall. Woods is nearly to the middle. With one hand solidly on the rafter that divides the barn, he throws a decadent come-and-get-me smile.

Janie Lee, in the way of all Lost Boys, chooses that moment to step forward. One step. Arms at her sides. Two steps. Arms outstretched. I follow slowly, checking on her to the front and on Davey behind. He is sure-footed and lithe. I focus on Janie Lee.

The timber beneath our feet is old, several inches wider than a railroad tie, and uneven. Janie Lee must feel the slight give in the lumber, especially with all of us up here. She hits the quarter mark. Fifty's taking a breather in the middle, where Woods stood only moments before.

Everyone moves quickly, wanting this over with.

Fifty's on the other side of the support as she's grabbing on when I hear her say, "I can't believe you got me into this," and he says, with a low laugh, "You got yourself into this the moment you and the other two pieces of the trinity got Billie on the ballot."

I realize instantly that I was not supposed to hear this. I would not have heard this if I had been spaced apart from Janie Lee the way everyone else was spaced. But Fifty didn't see that I sneaked in close, worried, ready to steady her if I needed to.

"Fifty, shut up," Davey says from behind me.

My arm hair is on high alert. "What are y'all talking about?"

Janie Lee turns carefully to me, lips quivering. "It was nothing."

"We'll tell you when we're on the ground," Davey says.

"Yeah," Janie Lee agrees.

"No." I am emphatic. "You'll tell me now."

This is not the place to have an argument, particularly this argument. There is so much dead air between me and the tables below. Janie Lee has her arms snaked around the center post, but I'm standing on an eight-inch-wide death trap.

In my peripheral vision, Gerry and Thom stretch their necks with concern. "You all right?" Thom calls up.

I yell back that we are fine. Cool sweat slides by my ear. Woods and Mash are reaching the other side and hooting, unaware. I am silently imploding.

"I want an answer," I say.

Her mouth is a gun, firing very quiet, very painful bullets. "It wasn't anything," Janie Lee says.

But Davey, sliding closer, disputes her claim, firing his own weapon. "Woods, Janie Lee, and I talked to the committee about you. We thought it would help. After the fire."

"So they didn't pick me?"

"Well, of course they did," Janie Lee says.

"You three manipulated them." My eyes ping from Janie Lee to Davey. His arms jut out to his sides like frozen propellers. All that drumming, all that pent-up energy, and he has the nerve to be still now.

She gives the reason. "We all felt bad about the Hexagon of Love thing. We were trying to make it up to you."

"By pitying me?" Tremors attack my knees, work their way into my voice. "But I guess poor Elizabeth McCaffrey could never be a girl on her own terms. I should have known." And that's the real source of my shame. I am ridiculously stupid for not seeing that my nomination had Woods Carrington's name written all over it.

Janie Lee and Davey both give some version of "That's not what anyone meant," but there is nothing else to mean.

"Easy, Billie," Davey says, propeller arms stretching slowly to me.

My body is a rolling boil in this shitty barn pot. The stale barn air licks my nose. I am having an emotional earthquake. If I fall I won't land on hay. The world tilts. Chairs and tables shimmer like holograms. If I fall I will break things.

"Billie." Thom tries to calm me from just below; I suppose he has heard it all. If I speak—ask for help—the weight of words will tip my balance. My arms seesaw wildly.

A tear splats on a table below. My sunglasses shake away from where they were tucked in the front of my shirt. I don't know where they end up, only that I heard them land on something solid.

"Deep breath." Davey sounds as if he's inside my head. He stretches out a blurry hand. I am spinning. I try to make contact.

This slight adjustment wrecks my remaining balance.

I am falling. Time slows down. I don't scream. Or if I do, it's lost in Thom yelling and Gerry squealing. Davey grabs me—a mistake. My momentum is too strong and he's not anchored to anything.

We go over the edge, each of us throwing an arm around the beam. My chin slams into the wood. I bite my tongue, and lose my hold. I drop again. I am suspended by my fingertips, mouth and eyes exploding with fear. Falling is inevitable. And to think: I was worried about festivals and first dances. Janie Lee screams; Davey says, "It's going to be okay"; Thom's crashing below, as he upends tables and creates space: they are all so loud. So very, very loud. My head has gone quiet in preparation.

I fall first.

Davey is right behind me.

33

Having Thom Cahill as a friend is the luckiest thing that has happened, perhaps in my life. He breaks my fall without my breaking him. But even Thom Cahill cannot be in two places at once. No one catches Davey.

Thom and I are heaps on the barn floor. There is copper liquid swirling in my mouth. When I touch my fingers to my tongue, they come away red. I move my jaw back and forth, making sure it isn't broken from where I hit the beam. My elbow collided with Thom's massive shoulder at some point. I am already sore, but I can't pinpoint a particular source.

Thom is groaning, but not the scary kind. Beside us, Davey is making a terrible noise. Thom untangles himself from me. We stumble-crawl to Gerry, who is already at Davey's side telling him he'll be okay. There's a compound fracture in his arm, three inches above his wrist, that I can hardly bear to look at. He absorbed the majority of the shock with a tuck and roll, but the impact had to go somewhere. Gerry leans over his chest, blocking his view of the blood.

I rest my hand on his bandanna and sweep his hair backward. It is greasy from the game and stays wherever my fingers leave it. He closes his eyes when I touch him, and I wonder if it's from pain or relief. I can't be angry with him right now.

His head lolls toward me. He's grimacing, but trying to be brave. "Are you okay?" he asks.

I nod and Thom distracts him with bad jokes. He winces, and Thom mouths to Gerry that we shouldn't let him move. But he's drumming the planks of the barn with his good hand, and sitting up on his own.

Woods jumps the last few rungs to the barn floor, the Hexagon hot on his heels. Janie Lee is a smeared mess of emotions.

I want to think: *Good for her.*

But really I think: *I'm sorry this all went to shit.*

"What happened?" Woods asks, removing his sweatshirt and draping it over the place where the skin is broken. Davey yelps, but Woods is talking about contaminants and keeping it as sterile as possible. Lifeguard talk, I'm sure.

"I knocked him down," I say.

"Don't listen to her. I was trying to be a hero," Davey tells Woods.

"Anything else hurt?"

"Everything hurts, but I don't think anything else is broken," Davey admits. His eyes are on Thom and me. "You two okay?"

We assure him we are.

"Let's get to the hospital," Woods says, but then Fifty says, "I already called 911. You're welcome."

"Asshole," Woods and I say together.

"What?" Fifty says.

Janie Lee has an answer for this. "Every person in town with a scanner will hear. And you-know-who will show up and report on this. Which is the last thing Billie's family needs."

Judith at the *Lamplighter* is married to her scanner. Rumor has it, her husband, Roger, said he'd divorce her if she didn't throw it in the lake and Judith said, "If it's you or the scanner, I'm picking the scanner." Because the most exciting thing Roger does in a day is move his toothpick from one side of his mouth to the other.

But with the ambulance ordered, we have no choice but to wait for the EMTs to arrive. We make sure we're outside the barn and looking innocent. The two twentysomething guys accept the answer of "horseplay" as a reason for the injury, but one says to the other, "We used to walk this damn thing when we were kids. Remember when Beau fell?" Davey climbs aboard with them, and as we watch the ambulance make the first turn toward the hospital, everyone downloads the shock of the situation at the same time.

"He'll be okay," Thom says reassuringly, heading toward the Audi so we can follow the ambulance. Only when I'm standing in front of the car do I realize the one fallibility of the Audi. There is a back shelf, but I cannot ride there. Which means I'm stuck with Woods and Janie Lee. In his truck.

I wedge myself against the door and close my eyes, silent. And they are silent. Everyone knowing what everyone knows, and no one having a clue where to begin. I'm glad they don't try. They've said enough. Did they all kiss me for pity as well? Did they all have a little meeting and say, "You know what, let's make Billie feel really loved and special?" Because thanks, no thanks.

We park near the emergency room, and Gerry strides over, warrior-like, cleans some of the blood from my face, and walks me arm-in-arm through the sliding glass doors. Inside, there is nothing to do but smell rubbing alcohol and sanitizer and avoid Judith's questions. She is here, as predicted, with her ever-present pen and yellow legal pad, desperate to make the story before the paper goes to print. "Why were you in the barn?" and "Were you present at the time of the injury, Ms. McCaffrey?" and "This is the second time you've called 911 this fall. Any comment on that?" and "You know, that barn has a reputation for its beam. Beau Wilson, ten years ago—he fell off the beam after a dare," she says.

I excuse myself, leaving her questions for Woods. He started this. He can finish it. I have blood on my shirt, and Gerry drags me to the bathroom and makes me swap with her. It's a small thing, but I'm thankful. Within thirty minutes, the room fills as the news spreads through town. A mishmash of details and drama will often make ambulance chasers of the whole town. My mom's rationale: "Well, when you know everyone, it's bound to be someone you know."

My parents show up and offer to pray. Dad's eyes flick to the broken skin and the purplish bruise that is spreading from my chin. He asks if I am okay with his eyes, as everyone makes a circle and bows their heads. I nod that I am. I pray along. Everyone has his or her eyes closed in a different way except me. Some squeezed painfully shut. Some resting. Some fluttering. Some leaking.

"Do they think he's dying?" Gerry inquires when the prayer is over and we return to our seats. "I mean . . . his arm is broken, not his neck."

I give her a weak smile. "This is just Otters Holt being Otters Holt."

"It's very charming," she tells me.

John Winters arrives an hour later. By now a nurse has told us that Davey is doing fine. Mr. Winters is in his gym clothes, looking frazzled and afraid, like maybe he drove triple digits to get here. Mash sits up straight when his uncle appears. I'm straight-backing it too. As is Hattie, like there's a grenade in the waiting room. But he doesn't yell. He asks Hattie some whispered questions and takes a seat across the room. Which still makes everyone uncomfortable, but not as uncomfortable as we expected.

Janie Lee risks speaking to me. "Can we talk? Not here, though."

I let my eyes stay at her feet, as if she is undeserving of my eye contact. But really I am ashamed. Ashamed that she assessed me and found me incompetent. The exact opposite of who a Corn Dolly nominee should be.

"Please," she says, and I'm stirred to at least listen.

We move slowly away from the crowd because I'm too stiff to move quickly. We follow the white-tiled hallway, through multiple sets of double doors. Elevators are to the right, exterior doors to the left. She leads us into starlight and fresh air. A breeze knocks my hair loose from its pins, and she says, "You know I'm sorry."

I don't doubt this.

Thin wisps of clouds cover the nearly full moon. She thinks of taking my hand, but draws hers back. I know her. She's wishing for pockets. But the little shorts she wears are pocketless and she's forced to grip her own hands instead of mine. How can I read her body language at this level and have missed something so colossal?

"I do," I say, finally.

"We made a mistake, but we thought we were doing the right thing. Can you understand that?"

I nod. But my understanding the error doesn't change the error.

She has one more thing to say. "We all love the hell out of you, and I hope you love the hell out of us back. Or at least enough to forgive us." And then she kisses my cheek and goes back inside.

With the Hexagon, there have been many predetermined endings. So much of our time together starts with Einstein, followed by Woods saying *We will* about something, and us replying *Of course we will*. Most of the time, we get what we want by virtue of wanting it badly enough.

Can I blame them for doing what we've always done?

But not everything can be mapped on Einstein. Not love. Not self-esteem. Maybe not even Harvest Festivals.

My love is wily, guileful even. Uncontrollable. Maybe theirs is too.

"I don't know what will happen," I say to the sky.

And Thom, who has slipped up beside me, says a good friend thing. "You don't have to, McCaffrey."

Thom is sturdy, the kind of person you can fall twenty feet on. I say, "Thom, how do you feel about Octagons?"

He says, "I failed geometry," and we both laugh.

Four hours later, the doctors release Davey to the care of his parents.

As I fall asleep that night, I realize one last ironic thing: not a single one of us voted for the Corn Dolly.

34

Davey's Part

It started with a newspaper article, written by Judith, an ambitious and insecure reporter at the *Lamplighter*. Two color pictures—one of me in the hospital, one of Billie donating money at the pitcher's mound—are positioned beneath the headline: LOCAL TEENS: HELPING OR HURTING? The bold, smaller line below says: *Should the youngest Corn Dolly nominee in history be disqualified?* The subsequent article has pictures of a Bible, meant to represent Big T's. Judith has interviewed someone present at the Fork and Spoon the morning we set this thing in motion. Someone who rightfully questioned the authenticity of our claims.

Our threesome marches up the library sidewalk and

through the plain glass door. There's a Save the Harvest Festival flyer taped to the inside bulletin board and an ad for an upcoming chili supper at Community Church. The Marshall County Library: Otters Holt Branch is a festive little place—festive as any building with that many brown items can be. Brown shelves, brown carpet, brown walls. Even the two librarians have brown hair and brown eyes. I wonder if it's in the job description. Nashville's libraries have gone white and modern, but this reminds me of Waylan Academy's reference section. I wish Thom were here to see me try this thing. He'd look up balls in the Oxford Dictionary and read a false definition that included my name.

But Thom is not here, and I have Woods and Janie Lee as my seconds today. The Harvest Festival committee is meeting one last time. Topics on the docket: Billie's candidacy and discontinuing the festival. We know this courtesy of Abram, who went on a bowling date with Martha Bittlebee. As Woods said, "He rang me up last night and told me the scuttlebutt." Woods said he used the term "snookie" in the description of Martha, and "Lord-a-mercy" in the description of the committee. Basically, we have a seventy-five-year old informant who is saying if we're going to act, we need to act now, and he's willing to put snookie on the line for the matter.

The latest issue of the *Lamplighter* is spread in front of every member. Twelve in total. Judith sits two chairs down from Ada May Adcock. She has punchy eyes that remind me of a grasshopper's.

Woods has promised I can do the talking, since I did so little of it when he and Janie Lee formulated and executed this half-cocked plan. I very carefully avoided any form of painkiller this morning so I would be better suited to the task. My arm is throbbing, but that's not where my mind is.

The committee doesn't know what we're here to say, only that we've interrupted their sacred gathering. No one seems happy about it. Several eyes drift accusingly toward Martha, who has the reputation of a large mouth.

I set Big T's Bible on the table and begin when Ada May flourishes her arm, as if we are taking up precious time and should be snappy with what we came here to say. Wilma Frist slides the Bible in front of the paper and begins to thumb through the tissue-thin pages. I try not to get distracted by Big T's ghostlike presence in this room.

Without going into detail, I paint them a picture as if I am back in debate club and this is my opening argument.

"We have a friend. Her name is Billie. You probably know her," I say, because they all do. "But . . . do you know she is the sort of person who will be a pallbearer at your funeral, who jumps into snake-infested water, who makes Book Dollies and newspaper couches, who prays, who cleans up elementary schools, who sticks by her friends, even when it costs her public embarrassment?"

I let that land in their hearts.

"She is an atypical candidate," I add, and then address the paper, picking it up and pointing at the large Times New Roman font. "But she deserves to be a nominee. Even if she doesn't win."

"But what about the fire?" someone in the corner says.

"I started that," Woods says. "It was an accident, but it was all me."

"And the stunt at Vilmer's Beam?" someone else presses.

"That was me," Janie Lee offers.

"Typical," Judith mumbles, and then gets down to a serious interrogation. "Mr. Winters, did you or did you not lie to Ada May and Wilma about her being in that Bible?"

Everyone except for Wilma leans their bifocals in our direction.

"That was me again," Janie Lee says.

"It was both of us," Woods says. He touches Janie Lee's hand for support. He can't bring himself to look around the room at so many of his friends.

Before anyone throws another question at us, I say the rest of what I came here to say. "I knew my granddad well enough to say that if he thought this was the last Harvest Festival, he would never disqualify Billie McCaffrey. And what I don't understand is why this group would waste time on this discussion rather than putting your full attention toward saving the Harvest Festival. You say you care about what Big T wanted, but do you? Because everyone in this room knows he loved that festival. As far as I can tell, only three of us in this room have done something about making sure it lasts."

Wilma Frist pushes the Bible into the middle of the table and says, "Luke 1:6, 'Elizabeth was a respectable woman.' The phrase is underlined. Look at the note," she tells the committee. They stand. They gather. They read.

We do the same.

Out to the side of Luke 1:6, Tyson Vilmer wrote Billie McCaffrey's name.

Holy hell. None of us saw that coming.

"It might not say Corn Dolly, but it might as well," Ada May declares.

And everyone nods.

No one more than Woods Carrington.

We leave the library knowing she might not win, but she won't be disqualified.

35

There are three things I have always loved about fall in Otters Holt.

The smell.

When I was younger, Grandy had a stellar imagination. She claimed that Otters Holt had weather fairies. Allegedly, the fairy folk poured gallon jugs of Downy fabric softener over a herd of John Rexler's cattle to make the smell. She then claimed Gene built his old windmill just for the expediency of spreading Aroma-cow over the county. This audacious image returns whenever I take a deep breath of pollen. I love Grandy for it.

The safety.

Small towns have invisible domes that keep the rest of the world out (and most of their people in). We'll happily tell others what they're missing. Playing outside, unlocked doors, stopping at a neighbor's house for a glass of water. We'll even argue we know what fun is and you don't. Like watermelon hooch or driving a tractor when your parents take away your car privileges.

Last but not least . . . I love this one perfect day of fall . . . the Harvest Festival.

I'm thinking about these three things as I sit on the rug in Dad's office, running my finger down the spines of old concordances and commentaries. They are the heaviest books we own. I loved them as a child. Not for their content, but because they made the best mazes for my toy cars. I whiled hours away on this rug. I'd been happy then, and Dad had been happy with me.

I ask what the deacons are saying and he tells me, "I am less concerned about deacons than I have ever been."

One week before, I would have been happy with this news. But the deacons aren't talking *to* him because they've switched to talking *about* him. Church leaders are not like tides. You can't set your clock to high and low a week or month in advance. They take a notion, and they turn quickly, suddenly. And once they have . . . there is very little turning back.

"Where will we go?" I ask.

"There's a camp position open in Florida. I've talked to the search committee," he says.

"And Mom?"

"She's okay if you're okay," he tells me. "She can paint anywhere."

He tries to sound brave, but his voice is thick, his tone heavy. I don't leave the floor for a long time, and when I do he says, "I'll make sure you get a new garage. No matter where we end up."

This kindness, this support, gives me the courage to leave the house and bike to town to meet Davey. From the elementary school roof, we watch a group of volunteers finish transforming Vilmer's Barn into a gathering hall— moving around the same tables and chairs Thom upended last Saturday. Men stand at a smoker the size of a tiny house while another crew unloads the dance floor in sections. It is not yet eight a.m., and the smell of barbecue is like an itch that demands to be scratched. Despite the October wind, the back of Woods's shirt is soaking wet. He has been working for at least an hour. I take photos of everything. I store these memories.

Today, no matter what, something in my life changes. Woods has apologized to me, and he has assured me that the guilty trio went to the committee with the truth. He has shown me Big T's Bible. While that made me feel marginally better, I'm still expecting to be disqualified tonight. There's the fire and the barn and the lies.

If I'm not disqualified but I lose, there is a very good chance we are moving to Florida anyway. I couldn't bear to ask Dad when. Before graduation? Before Christmas?

If I'm not disqualified and I somehow win, I will have to pick a dance partner.

Another line in the sand.

No one, not even Woods, is convinced that what we've raised is enough to keep the Harvest Festival alive. A good thing is dying. Einstein has failed us. More money could be raised over the next year, but the committee is measuring commitment. The mayor told Woods, "It's a big undertaking, son," as if Woods hadn't just pulled off the KickFall event.

This is Davey's first time on the elementary school roof. It wasn't easy getting him up here safely with his arm, but I'm glad that if everything is going away, we were here together smelling the Downy barbecue air and wishing we could freeze time.

"Come on. Let's go help," Davey says.

"Do you want to come with me to pick up Mr. Nix at three o'clock?" I ask. The gentleman originally wanted a ride at five o'clock, but he has called three times to move the time forward. I suspect that I'll have him in some vehicle by noon. That man could charm the pants off a tailor.

Davey offers to drive, and the day passes too quickly. As an act of loyalty, the Hexagon is attending the dance together. We join a game of Wiffle ball. We eat pumpkin pie. There's a dunking booth and inflatable games. I take Tawny Jacobs a popcorn ball, and she says nothing of the fact that I'm wearing ratty jeans and a T-shirt. I receive a triple-pat hand touch and a "Thank you." She probably can't eat the popcorn ball with her dentures, but if I'm leaving Otters Holt, I figure I owe her something for all those days of racing her perfect white fence lines.

Woods and Janie Lee play on the stage for an entire hour, and Mr. Nix claps along. I am shocked that the time is now five o'clock. I have opted not to change clothes. I only slip on the plaid shirt I've had tied around my waist and knock some dust from my boots. The best boots in the world. That's good enough for me.

"Now, you two are going to dance, right?" Mr. Nix asks Davey and me.

"Don't you worry, Mr. Nix, I'll make sure this girl gets a dance," Davey tells him.

Gerry and Thom—who have driven in for the festivities— feed Mr. Nix more pumpkin pie than Kevin, his nurse, thinks is healthy. Gerry's smitten with the man, telling Thom, "You'd better treat me right or I'm leaving you for Mr. Nix."

By the time the Corn Dolly candidates are encouraged to take the stage, Mr. Nix has forgotten what a Corn Dolly is. "It's a special corn husk, Mr. Nix," I say.

"Oh, right. Insignificant little thing, yes?"

Coming from anyone else this would be a slight. Davey says, "Yes, sir. But not to the ladies who win."

"Do you know any of them?" Mr. Nix asks me.

"I know all three."

"You must be very proud."

"Yes, sir," I say, and make my way to the stage. Unlike at the football game, I am on time.

The mayor hushes the band with a wave. The town stands in reverence. In a panoramic glance, I realize how flat everything in this town is. There are only one- and two-story buildings. Nothing taller than trees except for Molly and the dam. This place in Kentucky has only dips and ridges, no hills or valleys. We are at the highest point in our world.

The mayor holds the Corn Dolly high above his head.

Out in the crowd, Davey winks at me. Mr. Nix takes a nibble from a Little Debbie cake he's brought along. Janie Lee Miller looks right at me and smiles.

"Well, Otters Holt, it's that time," the mayor says. "Years and years stand at attention as we look to these three women and the most sacred award of our town." He talks about each of us, what he's observed, why we are worthy—a much better speech about me than at halftime—and the strength of this vibrant town to survive heartbreak and loss with the tools of community and love. By the time he finishes with his introduction, I'm not sure if he's described Otters Holt or Heaven.

Fifty's leaned over to Mash, probably saying as much. I imagine Gerry telling him to "hush his face."

"I had the privilege of counting the votes myself. We've never had better voter turnout. I can only assume that is thanks to the hard work of some young people who spearheaded the KickFall and revitalization project at the elementary school. I want to thank them, and each of these three candidates."

I spot my father near the stage. His shoulders are back, chin up. Even in his neat button-up and jeans, he is a man of faith, of principles. He does not look like a man who will easily wear swimming trunks at a youth camp in Florida. He nods at me for the moment of truth.

The mayor says, "And the recipient of this year's Corn Dolly is . . . Mrs. Tawny Jacobs."

I am glad she finally won.

It is a loss for my family, but I think of Fifty's stick drawing and Einstein. How he said, "I was just dicking around." Me winning was always a joke. But Woods must still be disappointed. I am not disappointed. This is exactly what I expected. My dad is kissing my mom's cheek, accepting a different future for our family.

I stand there, clapping for Tawny, realizing I'm relieved I didn't win. Because it would not have been fair. I'd rather be sad than ashamed.

Tawny Jacobs walks to the microphone, accepts the Corn Dolly from the mayor, and says, "I always wanted one of these." The crowd chuckles. "Or at least, I always thought I did. You know what they say, you know you don't really love something unless you learn to give it away. Elizabeth McCaffrey, will you come up here and join me?"

"What did she say?" I ask Caroline.

Caroline says, "I believe she's giving you a Corn Dolly."

I join Tawny at the microphone and she passes me the Corn Dolly. "I happen to have it on good authority that the margin of vote separating me from this beautiful young lady is four. And if I recall the night of the voting correctly, you and your friends were at the hospital and were unable to vote."

I cover my mouth with my hand, shocked.

"You deserve this," she tells me. And where no one can hear, she whispers in my ear, "Now, ask your girl to dance."

I recognize the precise tone. It is the voice I heard across the sanctuary. The one that urged me to forgive myself.

The crowd is stunned by her Corn Dolly gift. I am stunned by her words.

Across the field, Fifty and Mash catcall and whistle. The Hexagon calls out above all the rest. Janie Lee jumps in celebration with Woods.

I thank Tawny. I try to give the doll back. But she will have nothing of this.

I find myself in front of the microphone, and everyone asks for a speech. I say, "I wouldn't be on the stage without my friends and family."

"Name your dance partner," calls the mayor.

It is time to kick off the last Sadie Hawkins celebration. I look at Tawny and she gives me an encouraging nod.

The town is satisfied with this turn of events. "The preacher's daughter," they say. "I did love my Book Dolly," they comment. "She's a good Corn Dolly to end on," someone says in the front row.

I wonder if they mean that. Because I'm about to do the most unorthodox thing ever done at an Otters Holt Harvest Festival.

This thing between Janie Lee and me isn't a picture on Einstein or a bullet point from Woods. We're sloppy and disorganized, organic. Davey is pointing at her, mouthing, "Do it!" and I know he understands that I'm not choosing between them, but creating an opening in this town. The freedom Thom gave him. That Tawny Jacobs gave me. And if Tawny Jacobs can bring herself to understand, then there is hope for change.

For less fear in kids like me.

"Janie Lee Miller," I say bravely, "will you come up here and dance with me?"

36

The crowd parts, their expressions unreadable. A few scoff, but most just get wide-eyed and watchful. There is no way to know how they will respond when the band plays.

My parents have been absorbed by the crowd. I suspect I know what Dad's thinking: *Dammit, Billie.* Because I was so close to doing something the easy way.

I am marching to the platform, consequences be damned. Janie Lee is marching toward me. We are both smiling at each other.

It feels as though flint is striking steel inside my cheeks. She beats me to the dance floor, arms outstretched. The band strikes a chord. And the decision is made.

The crowd claps. They stomp feet and call moves—"do-si-do"— as they have always done. We are sponges for the music, taking it, keeping it, reveling in it, as we step in time to the beat. Square dances were asexual before the term existed, but we are still very close. And no one seems to mind.

In a moment when our hands touch above our heads in a bridge, she asks, "Aren't you worried what people will think?"

"Yes," I say. She is a whirling dervish who is gone and then back again before I can add, "But I'm trying not to care."

She has been trying not to care her whole life, because she is a Miller, and that's the way it is to be born a Miller. Her smile squeaks. I don't hear it—I can't hear anything except the music—but that's the smile that squeaks.

I must be staring and flat-footed because she says, "Dance, Billie."

We arm turn. Reverse. Another arm turn. Do-si-do. My arm hooks around her elbow for a swing.

"I'm glad you forgave me," she says.

"How could I not?" I say.

We settle into the dance, the steps coming easily—years piled on years of Harvest Festival experience. We are weight-less as we dance through decades of memories. Nearby, Woods hooks an arm around Mash and they gallop toward us like wild horses. Two boys dancing. Two girls dancing. No one cares. It is the very nature of a square dance to dance with everyone. We promenade and wave at Fifty to join us. This isn't a Fifty-approved event until Gerry drags him forward. Davey and Thom are here, having fought their way to us from mid-crowd.

The town cracks open like one of Tawny Jacobs's pecans.

Everyone dances, nearly everyone smiling and laughing, just as they have always done on this night.

This is how we grew up. Thirty minutes of square dancing followed by something a little more honky-tonk. Fifty will end up drinking beer from a Solo cup, Mash will throw up pumpkin pie, and it'll take me two washes to get the straw from my hair. But for now we listen as the mayor calls steps and the band unleashes more fiddle than seems possible. The Hexagon becomes heart-shaped.

We have almost danced our way to Mom when Wilma Frist and Ada May Adcock try to hush the band and storm the microphone. The music still plays and people keep moving, but their eyes are on the stage. Wilma Frist is the size of a toothpick beside Ada May; they look like a comedy routine from the sixties. Ada May pecks at the microphone, and yells, "Keep dancing. We just wanted to say, we've had a donation of five thousand dollars come in, which means, we don't care what the mayor says, we're doing the Harvest Festival next year."

There have been many cheers already tonight. None as loud as the one that follows this announcement. I feel like Cindy-Lou Who from *How the Grinch Stole Christmas*. I found a way to live with the festival being gone, but now it's all come back better than ever because we had to fight for it.

I locate Woods. He gives me an innocent shrug, which I disbelieve. He knows something. Woods didn't donate five thousand dollars, but he's too damn smug to not be involved. He wanted to have fun with a church microwave. He did. He wanted me to win the Corn Dolly. I sort of did. He wanted to save the Harvest Festival. And, uh, yeah, he did. His expression tells me that he's going to spend the next year of his life turning Judith at the *Lamplighter* or some unsuspecting individual into next year's candidate. He'll be mayor before he can legally drink.

I'll vote for him.

Mom is next to me now. She kisses my cheek and I pretend to wipe it away. We both laugh, and I suppose she's about to say something cheesy when Dad looks at Janie Lee and asks, "May I cut in?"

Janie Lee puts my hands in my father's, and he spins me away from Mom and my friends. I brace myself. *What was I thinking? Have I heard nothing he said? Do I care about my family at all? How do I feel about Florida?*

I have all his angry expressions on file, but this isn't one of them. In its place, something imperceptible. Wide eyes, closed mouth, whole head sitting crooked on his neck like he's watching an alien land a ship in the church parking lot. He says a curious thing. "I'm proud of you, Billie." From his pocket he takes one of my Book Dollies. "This is why *they* love you, but what you just did—following your gut, your heart—when you know it's not popular, that's why *I* love you. Don't forget that. Even when I do."

"Thanks, Dad," I say, and I realize it has been a very long time since I thanked him. For anything.

"No, thank *you*," he says, and kisses my forehead.

Gratitude: it's a good starting place for us. No matter where we end up. Everyone dances with everyone. But I won't forget this dance with my father. The one that makes the dance with Janie Lee even more special.

I am with Davey now, promenading, and suddenly I'm very relieved and very tired. I've been sprinting a marathon for a month and a half, and it has settled in my bones.

"Want to get out of here, Corn Dolly Queen?" he asks.

I've swallowed bite after bite of town all day, and I am as full as I would be after Thanksgiving dinner. "Yes," I tell him.

I look around, but the rest of the Hexagon has scattered themselves throughout the festival. We walk to the Camaro. I text Janie Lee and the Hexagon; he texts Gerry and Thom. We tell them to bring themselves to the garage after they're done dancing. Davey drives to my house, where we collapse on the Daily Sit.

Shadows fold over us. Guinevere nods her approval. The remnants of Belle and Beast lie like discarded snakeskins in the corner. Davey spots a package wrapped in brown craft paper with his name on it, like the one he brought me after the funeral. "What's this?" he asks.

"A gift to make up for knocking you off a beam."

I help him rip the paper.

He lifts a Batman mask circa Halloween 2007. The mask has not fared well in the summer heat—the stick-straight nose is melted against the cheek plate. It is the one I was wearing the first day we met. When I sucked at Wiffle ball and he thought

I was a boy. He laughs and I say, "I found it in the garage this week when I was cleaning out drawers. "Just in case you need a reminder—"

"That girls can do anything?"

"Well, something like that," I say. "It was you, wasn't it? The money."

"Where would I get five thousand dollars?"

I take the Batman mask from his lap and toss it playfully at his face. "Five years of costume winnings?"

His answer: "I never expected to love this place again."

I am silent then. Eyes searching around my garage at all the unfinished things that I love. Because that's this town too: unfinished, imperfect. My things have all surprised me in some way. They are like Tawny Jacobs, who danced with me tonight and told me about her best friend, Rachel Morgan. "Don't count people out," she told me. And I promised her I never would again.

I look everywhere but directly at Davey, because if our eyes snap to attention—blue on brown—this night will become something else, and I don't want that right now. I want to enjoy the low-grade hum of something left on in the corner—maybe a Bluetooth speaker from early this morning and the smell of epoxy from a spot in the floor and hayfields drifting in off the wind.

The garage door is up, and there's a full view of my driveway and the fields that lie beyond. It is vaguely light; the sky is a deep ocean blue, the moon a white rising ball. There's a dead tree along our fencerow. When I look directly through those branches, I see the very tip of Molly the Corn Dolly's illuminated yellow head.

"I never expected to love *that* thing," I say.

And Davey sees what I see. He says, "No one does," and we both laugh.

I take off my boots. He removes his high tops.

And then we get out the glue and newspapers and make a couch until the others arrive with an entire pumpkin pie and eight forks.

THE SHORT PART

after

PART THREE

No legacy is so rich as honesty.
—WILLIAM SHAKESPEARE

EIGHT MONTHS LATER

I rap three times on the youth room door.

Mash ushers us inside, peeling Twizzlers apart. Dad lied. He swore we'd never get a lock-in again, but he has folded, buying us pizza and mint chocolate chip ice cream. There's a *Happy Graduation, Class of 2017* banner hanging in the hallway.

We've been threatened and warned within an inch of our lives. Threats and warnings we ignore with marvelous gusto. This time, we have better intentions. And this time, there are no microwaves. Dad made sure of it.

Janie Lee and I sneak out the moment the coast is clear, this time with her leading the way. I tell her with moves like that, I'll give her a tombstone inscription. *Janie Lee Miller, born 2000—d.? IN LOVING MEMORY: Acquired Balls Along the Way.*

She shoves me in the butt with her UGG.

I take up residence on the floor below Janie Lee's papasan—Davey has saved me a pillow stack—and we all wait for Woods to set Einstein in its cradle. He has promised this night will be our favorite Einstein the Whiteboard Meeting of all time. I kick things off with the same old joke. "Let's start with glads, sads, and sorries, and then a prayer."

"Ha, ha, *ha*." Fifty launches another pillow at my head. He quickly adds, "I'm not going out for vodka. And you"—he slaps Mash on the back—"aren't throwing up. Gag-free night, you hear me?"

"Evolution is possible," Davey whispers in my ear.

Fifty's not the only one sporting a change. Woods offers the marker to Janie Lee and says, "Gather round, children, the lady has something to say."

Janie Lee flips the board around for our viewing pleasure. At the top, in her handwriting, are these words: WAYS TO GET FIFTY A CORN DOLLY.

Davey chuckles. Mash outright loses his cool.

"Oh, hell no," Fifty says.

He is up, tackling Janie Lee to the carpet before she reads the last word. This is the invitation. Everyone piles on. Laughing. We *are* a love sandwich.

I pry the marker from her nimble fingers and wiggle my way free of the body mountain. While they are still unraveling themselves, Fifty farts, Mash asks if anyone brought Peeps, and Woods tells everyone to "shush or we'll be found out." Neither Janie Lee nor Davey moves from the bottom of the pile.

I abscond to the couch with Einstein and write a new goal: WAYS TO BLOW UP EINSTEIN.

Everyone stares bug-eyed at Woods, waiting for a reaction. I have thrown down the gauntlet. His left eyebrow is up in the Canadian border. He smirks. He says, "Five bullet points, McCaffrey, and the marker is yours forever."

"I could do five bullet points in my sleep," I taunt.

We all laugh when Brother Scott McCaffrey knocks on the door and tells us, "If you're going to blow up the board, do it on your own time, and for the love of all that's holy, not at church."

Billie McCaffrey, born 1999—d. never. IN LOVING MEMORY: She can't be contained.

ACKNOWLEDGMENTS

Kelly Sonnack, Rosemary Brosnan, Alyssa Miele—there are no words to adequately express how thankful I am to travel this road with you. As a human, as an author, you make me better. You helped me be brave enough to tell *this* story.

To the entire team at HarperTeen—especially Bethany Reis, Maya Packard, Olivia Russo, Bess Braswell, Heather Daugherty, and Erin Fitzsimmons—you continue to make my dreams come true. That is no small task. Thank you. Thank you.

Patricia Riley, Maggie Stiefvater, Sarah Batista-Pereira—this book would not exist without your wisdom, investment, and care. Thank you.

David Arnold, Ruta Sepetys, Erica Rodgers, Kristin Tubb, RaeAnn Parker, Paige Crutcher, Lauren Thoman, and Holly

Westlund—no author could ask for better critiquers and friends.

It can be a perilous thing to be an author. One of the best safeguards is a great community. Here are some of the people who shepherded my life through the writing of this book: Victoria Schwab, Brenna Yovanoff, my Nashville taco crew, Batcave 2014, Christa Desir, Alina Klein, Sharon Cameron, Kate Dopirak, Joy Hensley, Brooke Buckley, S. R. Johannes, Myra McEntire, Stephanie Appell, Skywalker, Tessa Gratton and Natalie Parker, Julie Murphy, Bethany Hagen, Katie and Leah, Madcap Retreats, Midsouth SCBWI, Parnassus Books, Fannie Flagg (for giving me Idgie when I was a teen), and all the amazing teachers and librarians and booksellers who have been so supportive (especially Julie Stokes and the SEYA crew).

Mom, Dad, Matt, and my whole wonderful family—I love you so much. Thank you for everything. Carla and Christa, you are evergreen. This one was for you.

To the readers—you will always be my better half.

JOIN THE Epic Reads COMMUNITY

THE ULTIMATE YA DESTINATION

◀ DISCOVER ▶
your next favorite read

◀ MEET ▶
new authors to love

◀ WIN ▶
free books

◀ SHARE ▶
infographics, playlists, quizzes, and more

◀ WATCH ▶
the latest videos

www.epicreads.com